About Moss.

Moss is a literary journal of Northwest writing. Founded in 2014 and published online three times annually, *Moss* is dedicated to exploring the intersection of place and creative expression, while exposing the region's outstanding writers to a broad audience of readers, critics, and publishers.

Moss.

Volume Two.

M. A publication of Moss.
http://mosslit.com

Twitter: @mosslitmag
Facebook: facebook.com/mosslit
mosslit@gmail.com

Cover photo © 2016 by Alex Davis-Lawrence
Additional photo credits: see page 241.

Printing by Bookmobile Printing Services
ISBN: 978-0-9969379-1-7

Printed in the United States of America
1   3   5   7   9   10   8   6   4   2

Contents.

Introduction   1

Fiction

Sinkhole, Leyna Krow   3

Summer 1984, Sonya Chung   9

The Widower Muse, Michael Upchurch   71

Don't Worry, Anca Szilágyi   107

Alabama, Kjerstin Johnson   165

Unplace, Chris McCann   217

Interviews

Mitchell S. Jackson   47

Alexis M. Smith   113

Amanda Coplin   145

Elissa Washuta   185

Non-fiction

The Monolith, Eric Wagner   31

Non-fiction (continued)

The Jimmy Report, Tiffany Midge   125

Senior Time, Kelly Froh   137

Splitting the Sun, Gina Williams   161

This is Meant to Hurt You, Leah Sottile   199

A Multiplicity of Gray, Monet P. Thomas   211

Contributors   237

Photo Credits   241

Acknowledgments   243

Our landscapes may be strange—and they are dramatically variable from one mile to the next—but the stories that run through them are universal.

Alexis M. Smith

Introduction

Connor Guy and Alex Davis-Lawrence, Editors

It should be said, at the outset, that all of the work contained in this volume was completed before 2016's disastrous presidential election—before the danger of Donald Trump's presidency changed the paradigm of how art can, and must, engage with politics. How, then, are we to read the stories and essays collected here? Even the pieces from Issue 6, completed just weeks prior to election day, feel as though they were created in a world profoundly different from the one in which we live now. Is exploring the intersection of place and literary expression still as essential and productive as it was in the past? Will it bolster or distract from our practice of resistance?

At *Moss*, we believe that place is about more than just physical geography; it also encompasses our political, cultural, and social environment. In that sense, place remains as vital as ever in the era of Trump. Whether speaking of refugees fleeing brutal violence or of marginalized communities trying to survive within the United States, the right to freedom, safety, and opportunity seems inextricably tied to where we're from, where we're permitted to live, where we can find shelter—where we're allowed to belong.

In this bleak era—in which we face an adversary who is intent not only on dismantling our public institutions, but also on undermining our very sense of truth—literature has a critical role to play. Just a few short years ago, Northwest literary icon Ursula K. LeGuin warned that "hard times are coming, when we'll be wanting the voices of writers who can see alternatives to how we live now, can see through our fear-stricken society . . . to other ways of being, and even imagine real grounds for hope." Those hard times are here, and LeGuin's prescient call to action has gained new urgency. "Resistance and change often begin in art," she continued. "Very often in our art, the art of words."

It's the hope of many artists that their work will stand the test of time, and the work we've collected here has been very quickly put to that test; it was written in one era and will be read in another. But it's also become essential that our work stands the test of now—that it speaks effectively to this political moment, this crisis, this resistance. Whether we've passed that test, we leave for you to decide.

—<o>—

Sinkhole

Leyna Krow

The realtor showed us the house on West Garland Avenue and insisted it had everything we wanted.

"Look," he said, "there's a fireplace, granite countertops, crown molding, and a large sinkhole in the yard."

My husband Alex and I laughed because we thought he was kidding.

"No, really," the realtor said.

We told him we didn't want a sinkhole. That was not an item on our list. We agreed on this with absolute certainty. Back then, we always agreed with absolute certainty.

"I know," the realtor said. "But the house is a steal. Way bigger than anything else you'll find in your price range."

He was right. Besides, size was what we wanted most: a home with more space for our ever-expanding brood of children and pets. So we bought the house and put up a fence around the hole to keep the kids from falling in and for a while after that, we didn't pay much attention to it at all.

But then, one night a few weeks after the move, I asked Alex how deep he thought the sinkhole was. He said he had no idea. We went to look. We climbed our new fence and I held a flashlight while Alex leaned over the edge.

"I can't see the bottom," he said.

I stood beside him and peered in. It was almost as if the light was being swallowed up by the hole, eaten alive. We agreed it seemed sinister.

Then the beam of the flashlight began to fade and soon disappeared entirely.

"Piece of junk," I said. Overcome by a childish impulse, I pitched it into the hole.

"That's sort of wasteful, don't you think?" Alex said. "It just needed new batteries."

No, I said. I told him it felt good to throw the broken flashlight. The feeling alone was worth the waste. Alex chuckled at this. Back then, he thought I was funny.

Inside the house, the flashlight was waiting for us. It was perched at the edge of the coffee table.

"What the fuck?" I whispered, not wanting to wake the kids.

"Seriously, what the fuck?" Alex whispered back.

I picked up the flashlight. I didn't know if I should be afraid or impressed. A minute earlier I had thrown it into a hole in our yard and now it was here, in the living room, on the coffee table. I turned it over in my hands to test its realness. I flicked the switch and the light came on.

"The sinkhole fixed it," I whispered.

"Wait," Alex said, and for a second I thought he was going to warn me to set the light down and back away—it could be dangerous. But he didn't. What he said was: "Let's try something else to be sure."

He found a picture frame that had cracked during the move. I waited in the living room while he took the frame outside. In a moment, it was back on the coffee table just where the flashlight had been, the glass looking clean and solid. Alex returned and we inspected the repaired frame. We agreed it was incredible.

After that, we used the sinkhole quite often. We dropped in scuffed sneakers, forks with bent tines, books with torn covers. They all reappeared on the coffee table good as new. Soon the sinkhole became just another feature of the house we were grateful for, like the dishwasher and the walk-in closets.

We never considered the effect the hole might have on anything living. Not until the morning our oldest son, Jake, woke me to announce in a tear-ragged voice that something was wrong with his turtle. He was holding the turtle, named Bert, in both hands. I could see the creature was sick. I didn't want to take both boy and turtle to the vet only to hear bad news. So, I led Jake to the yard and helped him over the fence to the hole.

"Put Bert in there and it will fix him," I said.

I thought Jake would protest, but worry for his pet made him compliant. He set Bert into the hole and gasped when he disappeared. Back inside, he found Bert on the coffee table and ran to him. The turtle was much improved. But a pale of concern remained on Jake's little face.

"Is my turtle a zombie now?" he asked.

"No, of course not," I told him. "Zombies are dead things that come back to life. Bert was just sick. The sinkhole made him better."

As soon as I said those words—*The sinkhole made him better*—I felt a kind shiver run through me. Like I'd just found the answer to a very important question I hadn't even thought to ask.

I began to wonder what the sinkhole could do for me, if I put myself in it.

I wasn't sick like Bert. I wasn't broken like our clock radio. But I wasn't the best version of me, either. I was thirty-eight, my body damaged from childbearing, and before that from alcohol and hair dye and music that was too loud. The usual things. Adulthood wore down my character, too. I was impulsive and at times forgetful. No great crimes. But wouldn't my family be happier with an improved me? Wouldn't I be happier?

I suggested this to Alex one night and he said no.

"I like you the way you are."

I thought he was just being kind. Back then, we were always kind to one another.

"But wouldn't you like me better if I was better?"

"No, because then you wouldn't be you."

I didn't see this as the compliment he intended. I felt he was saying my essential nature was a flawed one.

Alex looked into my eyes and I could see the worry creep across his face.

"Please promise me you won't get in that sinkhole," he said.

"Why not?" I asked.

"Because it's weird. It's a weird thing to do."

I promised, but I couldn't help but see this conversation as evidence for exactly why I needed so badly to go through the sinkhole: My logic was flawed, my thinking strange. What kind of woman wants to put herself in a hole? I felt strongly that if I used the hole to make myself better, I would banish such weirdness. I would no longer be the sort of person who wished to get into holes.

Alex kept looking at me. I didn't say anything because I didn't want to lie to him. Back then, we never lied.

I felt ready to get in the hole that night, but chose to wait. I wanted to be certain I was doing the right thing. So, for the next week, I went about my life as my normal, flawed self. I went to work, I visited with friends, I fed, cleaned, and entertained my children. I was kind and agreeable and honest and funny with Alex, like always.

But in my head, I kept a list of each mistake I made, every error a more perfect me would have been able to avoid—a burnt pan of lasagna, a forgotten birthday, a child scolded too harshly. And so on. Normally, I might have chastised myself for these missteps and later recounted them to Alex so he could reassure me they weren't really so bad. But instead I hoarded them almost gleefully. They were the evidence against myself. I was building my case for the sinkhole.

I made a habit of visiting the hole before bed each night. I took my flashlight and, dressed in my slippers and robe, stood beside it, looking in. It was a meditative practice of sorts. I tried to think of nothing while

I did this—not my flaws, or what a flawless me might be like. I just stood and stared, letting the darkness of the cavern fill my mind with calm and hope. Sometime I was aware of Alex watching me as I did this, waiting at the bedroom window for me to finish my ritual. But he never said anything about it. Why didn't he say anything? What was wrong with me that my beloved husband could watch me do something that bizarre, night after night, and never feel capable of confronting me about it? Was I so fragile? So frightening? So beguiling?

Then one evening Jake went off for a sleepover and left me with instructions to feed Bert—what kind of veggies and how much. Of course I forgot. In the morning, the turtle gazed out at me from his cage with what I imagined to be a hunger-stricken look. *Never again*, I thought.

I went straight for the hole. As I climbed the fence, I wondered about my entry. Should I dive? Cannonball? No. Such actions would suggest a kind of playfulness. But this was not play. It was work—the work of repairing myself. I walked into the hole as if stepping off a curb. I tumbled over once in the dark air then I was seated, legs crossed, back straight (no more slouching for me!) on the edge of the coffee table, feeling calm and perfect. Like I was someone else entirely. So, Alex had been right, of course. I was no longer myself. But the new and better me didn't care. The better me was content to sit at the edge of the table, waiting patiently for Alex to come home so I could show him all the ways I'd changed.

—<o>—

Summer 1984

Sonya Chung

"Summer 1984" is an excerpt from the novel The Loved Ones, *published by Relegation Books in October 2016.*

—◁◦▷—

The boy was six, the girl nine. Their father, Charles Frederick Douglass Lee, was himself one of five children; each had looked after the next while Charles's mother worked night shifts and his grandmother worked days at the same corner store owned by a cousin. He'd come up fine and didn't believe in babysitters. It was his wife, Alice, who insisted the girl was not old enough to be left alone with the boy. "What if there's an emergency," Alice Lee said to Charles. She often made statements in the form of questions. She said "emergency" in a near whisper.

"She's a smart girl, she knows how to dial a phone." Charles favored the girl, loved her more, even; but he was careful not to show it as much as he might. Veda was dark-skinned, almost as dark as him, darker than the boy, but had most of her mother's features—heart-shaped face, gray eyes, celestial nose. She did have his full lips and bright, large-toothed smile, everyone said so. She had his dark, purplish gums, too; though no one said so. Veda's hair was dark brown, soft and wavy, but her mother didn't understand as well as her father what this meant, how lucky she was.

The boy, Benny, was light-skinned, but he had his father's thick eyebrows and prominent forehead. He was a big boy for his age and barreled around like a fullback, shoulders squared, hands balled into fists. He couldn't yet read, or wouldn't. Sometimes he still wet the bed. He'd bitten other children, more than once, and crashed full-force into anything in-progress that he hadn't himself started—a jigsaw puzzle, another boy's Lego house, his sister's My Little Ponies arranged for a pageant. Charles marveled at Alice's calm, even tones with both children. Sometimes he loved her for it, sometimes he hated her. Sometimes he wanted to slap the boy and shove his wife; sometimes the other way around.

Alice Lee was going back to work. She was a social worker and had found a position at a Korean nursing home in Silver Spring. She'd been home with the children all these years and was fortunate to get the job after being out of the workforce. Alice did have a nurse practitioner's degree—she'd gone to night school when Benny started pre-K—and the nursing home needed someone like her, who could communicate well enough with the Mexican service staff (Peace Corps in Chile), with the residents and doctors (DoD educational assistant, Yongsan Base in Seoul), and with the pharmaceutical and insurance people on the phone.

For weeks Charles and Alice argued over whether to hire a baby-sitter—"discussed," Alice would say—and in the end Charles gave in, mostly for the girl's sake. Why should she have to watch over the boy.

"There's a nurse at the home whose daughter could do it," Alice said. "She sounds *perfect*. Polite, responsible. Her mother has been with the home for many years."

So she's already arranged it, Charles thought. Of course she has.

"Her name is Lee," Alice said, like an offering, and with a chuckle. "Hannah—the girl—Hannah Lee."

A Korean girl. Charles didn't like it. Just as he didn't like his wife working at that nursing home. Did the mother of the girl know about him? Charles didn't have to ask. No way she did. Not yet. Alice would wait to reveal it, her *gamman-saram* husband—to the mother, to all her coworkers—after she'd proven herself trustworthy, likeable. His wife was a smart girl, too. Lee was likely a useful name to have around there.

Charles wasn't surprised: so many of them were named Lee. He'd gotten used to it in Korea, the bitter irony. The KATUSAs had found it especially amusing: *Lee-san*, they'd called him, though he generally didn't take it as friendliness.

Hannah Lee came by herself on a Saturday afternoon in late May to meet the children and be shown around. When the bell rang, Alice was in the backyard with the boy. Charles was scanning the scores and listening to WJFK sports; he got up from his recliner to answer.

The girl wore a navy T-shirt dress with a braided belt hanging below the waist, jelly sandals, and shiny lip gloss (in fact it was just Vaseline; her mother did not allow makeup). Her eyeglasses were perfectly round, her hair wavy and brown at the ends. Her legs were long, and she looked older than Charles had expected. Thirteen, Alice had said. Maybe it was her handbag, a square Gucci that was slung across her body and reminded Charles instantly of the fakes sold in Itaewon by the dozens to officers' wives. Or maybe it was the solemnity of her pale, rectangular face. When she smiled and introduced herself, it seemed to require effort, an awkward exertion. But it wasn't his black face that troubled her. Charles knew *that* look—he'd borne it over and again from Alice's friends and family. No, it wasn't that; it was rather the strain of nicety, a learned affect of cheerfulness that did not come naturally to the girl. Alice had apparently missed it on the phone the day before—*She sounds perfect*—and this knowledge gave Charles Lee a small burst of pleasure.

The phone rang just as Soon-mi squatted by the flowerbed with trowel and kitchen knife. She could hear it through the sliding screen door, and so could Chong-ho from across the small yard. The day was mild and still and overcast, and the deep ink-blue of the *Baptisia*—false indigo it was sometimes called—seemed to ring brightly, shockingly, along with the telephone.

It was late in the season to be dividing, but the forecast called for cooler weather and light rain tomorrow, Sunday, into Monday. There was space in the flowerbed that bordered the back of the house where a peony had been lost to an early spring storm (the gutter had come crashing down). Soon-mi thought she could divide and replant all three indigos, maybe finish the weeding she'd started earlier, too, before dinner.

Chong-ho looked to Soon-mi from the vegetable garden. Not with his eyes, but with his attention. The phone rang a second and third time.

Soon-mi stood and removed her gloves, laying them down along with her tools on the patio table. She slid the screen door open and stepped through.

Chong-ho looked up and saw Soon-mi's blue rubber slipper dangling from her foot. The slipper dropped to the doormat as Soon-mi disappeared into the house. Who could be calling, Chong-ho wondered, at this time on a Saturday. Probably one of Hannah's school friends. That girl who was always calling, the fat one with the brown skin and short skirt who talked too fast. She'd come after school with Hannah once but then never again. Maybe Soon-mi had said something, though likely not; Hannah would not need to be told. Chong-ho grimaced and went back to transplanting the go-chu.

During the week sometimes there were sales calls, but never on weekends. Soon-mi thought it could only be one person, and she let out an audible sigh when she heard James's voice—as if her wishing had made it so.

"Hi, *Ummah*." There was an echo, along with yelling and laughing in the background.

"James?" Soon-mi said. She'd raised her voice, and it cracked. "Why so much noisy?"

"Those are just my suitemates. I'm in the bathroom with the phone. Remember when I switched the long cord from your phone last time? It's the only way to have any privacy around here."

"Sweet? Mate?"

"Roommates, Ummah. I have two, I told you. They're okay. Just blowing off steam before exams."

"Unh. Exam. You have exam now. That's why you call today?"

"Exams are next week," he said. "I have study groups tomorrow, all day." There was a muffled bang, then the crash of aluminum cans hitting the floor. James covered the mouthpiece and hissed, "Hey, dickheads, knock it off."

Soon-mi waited.

"Sorry, they're just horsing around. Anyway. Um..."

They spoke for just a few minutes, as always. When he asked for Hannah, Soon-mi said she'd gone out, and didn't mention the babysitting job. It was a long story, and she didn't care to get into it; Hannah could tell him herself next time. And who knew how long it would last anyway. The American woman, Alice Lee—her children were old enough to be home alone, really.

"Tell her to call me sometime," James said. "Just, you know. Whenever."

"Unh, okay," Soon-mi said. She told him to make sure he ate well, not just ramen noodles, and he laughed, even though she wasn't making a joke. Then they hung up.

Soon-mi stepped back out onto the patio and retrieved her trowel and knife. As she pulled on her gloves she became thoughtful and laid the tools again on the table, then walked toward the far end of the yard, the sunny corner, where Chong-ho was putting the last of the go-chu seedlings in the ground.

"*Moh han-eun goon-yo?* What is it?" Chong-ho handed her a seedling, then proceeded to mix in the fertilizer he'd just sprinkled over the hole. Soon-mi cupped the ball of spindly roots in her orange gloves. She told her husband that James was fine and conveyed his reason for calling on a Saturday. Chong-ho clawed at the dirt in the bottom of the hole with both hands—he never wore gloves—making sure the plant food was deeply and evenly mixed.

When he was done, Chong-ho held out his right hand, which was dark with earth, and Soon-mi placed the seedling in his palm. "Hannah missed talking to him." The words formed themselves, and multiple meanings, from an uneasy place that Soon-mi knew well; though only as a kind of bodily thrumming. She couldn't have named it, not even to herself.

"Where did she go?"

Soon-mi was silent. She had not anticipated this question; that is, she had not considered how she would answer it. She had been distracted sendingHannah off. Of course Hannah's father would question the purpose of her having a job: they provided for her, she should be studying. "Out with a friend," Soon-mi said, and their eyes met briefly as Chong-ho stood to stretch his back. In that glance, Chong-ho was saying, *What you tell me is always truth enough*, and Soon-mi was saying, *I understand the nature of your trust.*

Chong-ho squatted again, and Soon-mi knelt next to him. He mixed in the plant food and set the seedlings in the holes. She scooped dirt and filled the gaps, then patted the soil. When they got to the last hole, Soon-mi said, "Hannah should call him. He has good advice for her, I think. He is becoming more responsible, concerned for the younger one."

Chong-ho said nothing. Soon-mi shifted her weight to achy ankles and hips, and brushed off her knees. As she turned to work on the *Baptisias*, Chong-ho raised his head and said, "She will be home for dinner?"

"Unh," Soon-mi said.

Chong-ho lowered his eyes, and with that, it was agreed: he would encourage Hannah to call her brother.

Soon-mi's slippers made a muted slapping noise against her socks as she walked toward the house. She would have time to divide and transplant only one of the false indigos. She worked from a squat, and when she plunged her trowel into the ground, loosening the root ball on all sides and then pulling up from the base of the stalks, she felt how deep and intricate the roots were; how they clung to the earth that fed them. She dug deeper, pulled firmly and evenly from the top, wiggling the plant from side to side. The roots loosened, and Soon-mi thought, Why *should* Hannah work for the American family? Soon-mi had made the offer to Alice Lee without thinking, though it seemed right at the time. She'd felt relief when the woman wrote down their phone number. Hannah would be occupied, looking after children. Soon-mi was not convinced this was a bad idea; nor a good one, exactly. The uneasy thrumming persisted.

The root ball came up, and Soon-mi fell back on her heels but maintained her squat. She laid the matted, gnarly thing in the dirt and eyed the knife, which she'd staked upright at the border where dirt met grass. She sighed. This was the part she didn't like. Always she had to remind herself, as she sliced through the bone-white roots and off-shoots like baby hairs, that she was regenerating, propagating, and not destroying.

It was the Saturday before Memorial Day, and Kenyon Street was lined with American flags. They shot out like saluting arms from the porch roofs of row houses. The flag on Charles and Alice Lee's four-bedroom brick was smaller than the neighbors'—colors dull and faded by comparison, material drab. In this way, the house stood out.

Hannah Lee walked east from the Columbia Heights Metro station along a sidewalk that was clean but badly cracked. Weeds and tree roots pushed up with a brute force that made her think of her crooked front tooth—how the baby tooth had hung on stubbornly until the permanent one had to come breaking through at an angle.

There were people sitting on every porch or stoop along the block—black people, mostly old people, a few babies and toddlers in their laps. They stared as Hannah walked by. She stared back. No one smiled. One little boy waved. Hannah was not frightened or nervous, though she had some awareness that perhaps she should be. She didn't mind—liked it even, a little, this being noticed.

The Lees' house was exactly mid-block. There was no one sitting on the porch or stoop, just a mess of bicycles and car/truck/train toys, and potted plants, flowers mostly, unkempt and clustered along the left end of the red-painted steps. Hannah liked the house right away, though she could not have said exactly why. She did think of how her father would have scoffed at the annuals in the pots—her parents grew only vegetables and hardy perennials, in large beds that they tended meticulously from March to November—and how her mother would have pursed her lips at the disorder.

Soon-mi had not asked to see the exact address; Alice Lee had told her, "a short walk from the Columbia Heights stop," but she had not said in which direction. Soon-mi assumed west, toward the park. Alice Lee was a white woman with a master's degree, after all.

Hannah rang the bell and waited. A man came to the door. He looked surprised, and he stared at Hannah, though in a different way from the porch and stoop people. Hannah did not mind this man's staring either, though after a few moments of silence she couldn't help but think of her brother, James, who—now that he was majoring in business instead of smoking pot behind the Burger King—had started calling her "spacey."

"I'm... Hannah. The babysitter." Something caught in Hannah's voice—a flatness swallowed her words. She had intended to be polite, and cheerful. She didn't know what had come over her: it was like when she had to read Ophelia's *Hey nonny, nonny* section in front of the class and she delivered it deadpan, even though she knew she was supposed to be dramatic.

The man was very dark, and big like an athlete. He had a broad, smooth forehead; wide Eskimo cheeks; a strong jaw, which hung slightly open. His eyes were round and shiny and black, like licorice jelly beans, and Hannah looked straight into the right one (his left), which she could just barely do without craning her neck. He was handsome, this man. She liked the word—much more than *cute* or *hot*—and enjoyed the pleasure of both beholding and thinking it. (*Pleasure*, on the other hand, was a word that Hannah would never have thought, or spoken.)

Charles blinked once. Hannah lowered her gaze to the many-colored flecks in his brown sweater vest, then to the crisp white of his T-shirt. Her eyes landed on Charles's collarbones, which pushed out just like the sidewalk's thick tree roots.

Hannah cleared her throat. "Mrs. Lee said... three o'clock." Her feet pressed hard into the concrete, her shoulders dropped from her ears. Charles lowered his chin, put one hand on his head as if to rub it, then stepped back from the door. He said her name and got it wrong—*Come on in, Anna*—and Hannah corrected him: "No, it's *Haa*-nah." The voice that came out this time was strangely familiar—it was the one she normally heard only inside her head. Not rude exactly, but absent the interrogative tone that all the girls had begun using.

The voice had raced out. Hannah wished she could chase after the words and smash them with her hands like ants, but then Charles Lee's hand came off his head, licorice eyes rolling up and smiling bright. "Sorry, right. Come in, *Haa*-nah." Voice warm and deep. Not deep like a tuba, but lighter, and a little sad, like a clarinet. Hannah stepped past, two long strides, and into the house.

Charles led Hannah through the kitchen to the back door. Hannah kept both hands on her purse. In new places she felt loose and awkward with her hands dangling at her sides; she always wanted to touch things, like a blind person groping for direction.

Charles opened the screen door and stepped out onto a cement landing. "Alice," he called, and motioned for Hannah to descend the steps. His voice had changed: it was both heavier and more floaty. Hannah watched her feet as she took each steep and slanted step. Charles disappeared into the house, the screen door crashing shut.

"No slamming!" A boy stood up from a crouch, sausage finger pointing up in the air.

Alice Lee was kneeling in the grass. She raised herself up without using her hands, brushed dirt from her denim pedal pushers, then nudged a bouncy blonde lock from the corner of her eye with a knuckle. "And no shouting, mister," she said.

The boy was Bennett, after Alice's maternal great-grandfather. They called him Benny. He grinned, slapped a chubby brown hand over his mouth, then frog-leaped to another corner of the sandbox, toward a yellow dump truck. Noisy, catastrophic collisions ensued. The boy was all hair, big and Brillo-y, the same burlap-sack color of his skin. He wore a T-shirt two sizes too big, shorts that went down to his calves. He was an ugly boy, and not a little frightening.

"You're Hannah," Alice said, smiling with her lips but frowning with her eyes.

It was an odd greeting; it made one feel caught out somehow.

Charles leaned on the kitchen sink drinking a Pabst and looking out the window. He felt for the girl. He watched his wife amble over in her cowgirlish way, reaching out her hand. The two were likely the same height, but Alice slouched slightly—or maybe it was just her sharp shoulders and short neck, it was hard to tell. Charles did not care to watch anymore. He went back to the scores, to his La-Z-Boy.

Out in the yard, Alice said, "So this is it," spreading her arms. "Did you have any trouble finding us?" Hannah shook her head no, said from Wheaton it was six stops and one transfer, and a short walk from the station, just as Alice had said. "Good, I'm glad it won't be a long commute for you. Makes everything simpler." Alice went on to describe the areas of the small yard and what each child liked to do there—Veda at the picnic table with her craft projects, Benny in the sandbox or on the climber. There was a trellis with thick brown vines growing all over it that looked like something out of a children's storybook. It was in fact a small fig tree whose branches had grown long and snakelike. "Hose play is fine, especially on hot days, but you should hold the hose for them, or else Benny gets a little wild."

"Should they be in swimsuits?" Hannah asked.

"Veda will want to change. Benny can just lose his shirt."

Hannah nodded.

"So Benny is six," Alice continued, as if pointing out yet another feature of the yard.

"Six and a quarter!" Benny shouted.

"Six and a *quarter*." Alice rolled her eyes, and Hannah pushed out a small laugh. "Veda is nine, ten in August. She's at a friend's house down the street. I'll show you the rest of the house and then you and I can walk over to the Mitchells' to pick up Veda. She's over there enough that you should meet them." Hannah nodded again. Alice Lee was clearly, thoroughly in charge.

After the tour, which was just a walk around the first floor, Alice told Charles they'd be back in a few minutes. Benny continued to accelerate, crash, and explode things in back. "When you can't hear him, *that's* when he needs checking on." It was not clear for whom the statement was meant, Hannah or Charles.

The front gate closed behind them; Hannah and Alice headed west to the Mitchells'. With her mind, Hannah looked back toward the house; with her eyes, she noticed Alice Lee's bouncy blonde hair. It was just the style she herself had hoped for when she'd gone for a perm. On Alice Lee, though, with her pointed shoulders and skinny legs, it looked somehow not-right—like movie-star sunglasses on a cloudy afternoon.

They walked in the opposite direction from the station—just two streets over, but a different neighborhood altogether. The sidewalks were wider, and even; the faces mostly white, and relatively young. On one side of the street the houses were very tall and lean—all brick, and without porches. Some of them looked like castles, with their bay windows and turrets. On the other side, the porch roofs were held up by beautiful white pillars. None of the houses on the Mitchells' street had chain-link fences.

Hannah thought how her father would consider all these houses inferior—attached to one another, with tiny yards. But Hannah liked them—the way she liked chess, which her friend Raj had taught her, and memorizing vocabulary and verb conjugations for Madame Glissant's French class. Anyway, she knew her father missed a lot of things; that he and her mother lived so much apart from others, and that they didn't—couldn't, somehow—see everything clearly.

Alice stopped in front of a fancy iron gate and let out a mysterious sigh. It was a tall porchless house with green double doors. They ascended the steps, and Alice rang the bell. "Karen's a pediatrician, so I never worry when Veda is over here on the weekends." Alice spoke in tight, confident tones, like a receptionist for an important person. "Amy is Veda's best friend, and they're young for sleepovers, but I allow it. Amy's a very sweet girl."

On cue, they heard the pitter-patter of small feet. A tiny, full-freckled girl pulled the door open with both hands.

"Hello, Amy," Alice said, leaning down as if she might pet her.

"We knew it was you," Amy Mitchell giggled. Her bare feet were cross-stacked on top of each other, one knee bent, in the manner of children who have to go to the toilet. She chewed on a strand of frizzy brown hair, the rest of which was piled elaborately on top of her head with a fistful of bobby pins. Sparkly pink earrings hung from her lobes.

"Hi Alice, come in!" a voice called from within. Alice helped Amy with the door, pushing her way inside.

"They're here!" Amy called.

"My, what pretty earrings," Alice said, reaching out with her fingertips.

The girl leaned forward so they could be properly admired. "We're playing makeover." Amidst Amy's freckles were glitter stars, sparkling around her eyes and cheeks.

Amy turned and pattered back toward the kitchen. Alice and Hannah followed. Alice fell behind Hannah, lingering to notice the new bamboo floors. The lighting was different, too—modern half-moon sconces led them down the long hallway. Karen Mitchell had a busy practice and was highly sought-after among the government set; she also published articles and taught at Georgetown. Her husband, Rick, was an estate lawyer.

"Hi, Karen. I guess we're a little earlier than I said." It was not quite an apology.

In the kitchen they found Veda sitting in a lacquer bar chair, legs crossed at the ankles. Her hair had been tightly French-braided and tied up in back. A rhinestone tiara circled her crown. Karen Mitchell leaned over her, applying blue eye shadow.

"Ta da!" The shadow was light and shimmery on Veda's dark skin. The girl sat perfectly upright, and with her hair pulled back so tightly her face looked both calm and alert. Against the shimmer of the blue shadow and the sparkle of the tiara, Veda's grey eyes turned translucent, shifty and complex like a crystal.

Hannah nearly gaped. The sight of Veda took her breath away, and for a moment, she saw not a made-up child in a stranger's kitchen, but an African princess.

"My goodness." Alice's tone was somehow both airy and taut. Amy giggled with her hand over her mouth.

"Oh, I hope you don't mind, Alice. I had a feeling this blue would just be spectacular on V. Do you remember wearing this stuff? God, the seventies!"

Alice smiled weakly. She'd never worn eye shadow in her life. Karen's thin pink T-shirt was sliding off her bare shoulder, pale and freckled like her daughter.

"These next, these next!" Amy was jumping up and down, holding a small black container with a clear plastic top. False eyelashes.

"Put those down, honey. Those are for another time, maybe. In a few years." Then Karen winked at Hannah. "Maybe when you're old enough to babysit."

"Oh, gosh, sorry." Alice's voice was looser now, but too loud. "This is Hannah, who I was telling you about. She'll be watching the kids after school."

"We have a babysitter, too," Amy said, twirling around on the ball of one foot. "She's sixteen, and she has big ones."

"Amy." Karen flashed her daughter a look, but she was smiling.

"Well, Hannah is thirteen, but she's very *responsible*."

Hannah flushed. Something had changed in the air. Karen Mitchell stepped back from Veda, who thus far had not said a word.

Veda blinked her eyes and climbed down from the chair, her head and neck held perfectly still. She reached for Hannah's hand. "You have to help me wash this off now," she said, as she led her new responsible babysitter to the bathroom. Amy skipped along behind, and Alice stared after them.

Karen cleared her throat. "They had a nice time."

"She always does," Alice said, remembering to smile.

"I thought I might have to run to the hospital and leave them with the sitter, but I'm so glad I was able to get someone to cover for me."

"Mm," Alice said.

"So Hannah seems nice," Karen said. "Very calm. How long has she been with you?"

"Oh, just today. It's her first day."

"Oh! My gosh. I didn't realize. I'm sure she'll be just great. And it's so terrific, Alice. You back to work. And using all of your... experiences, after all these years. I don't know if I could do it. If I'd stopped working when Amy was born. But you're so *brave*, and you've had so many interesting *adventures*. Remind me—you speak Korean, right?"

"Just a little."

"And is Hannah's English pretty good?"

Alice looked at Karen, whose linen miniskirt showed off her athletic thighs. Karen was turned away, gathering the makeup containers. Something hot and scratchy rose in Alice's throat. "Karen, Hannah speaks perfect English. Don't you have any colleagues at the hospital who are immigrants?"

Karen turned back with a quizzical look. She might have been considering Alice's question; she might have been considering Alice.

Alice laughed, a little too sweetly.

Amy came skipping from the bathroom to find the two women locked in silence. It was Alice who turned away first. "How's it going in there?"

"The soap," Amy said, "it's stinging her eyes."

"Oh, jeez, you need this," Karen said, reaching for a small blue bottle. "Here you go, pumpkin."

On the way home, Alice walked with her arm around Veda's shoulder and said to Hannah, "That Amy really is such a sweet girl."

It was the first day of summer. The children's summer. School was out, but Hannah still took the Metro to Columbia Heights station in the afternoons, as she had for the previous three weeks. Alice worked the 3-to-11 shift at the nursing home, which meant she was home until 2:30. "So it will just be an hour earlier every day," she had said, and Hannah said that would be fine. Her only other plans for the summer were to read *Le Petit Prince*—which Madame Glissant had recommended to her—and to swim every day, which she did at the pool in Silver Spring. In the fall, Hannah would start high school and intended to be the number-one seed in backstroke. Raj's brother Ravi had said that the girls' team *sucked*, and this, Hannah thought, boded well for her.

Alice did not ask what else Hannah would be doing when she was not watching Veda and Benny. But she did raise Hannah's wage by fifty cents an hour. "It's the least we can do. There must be so many other things a girl your age wants to be doing with her summer afternoons." It was a funny thing to say, Hannah thought—as if Alice Lee had some completely different girl in mind when she said it. But Hannah was happy for the raise; it was the first time she'd had her own money, and she was saving up. For what, exactly, she didn't yet know.

In the evenings, Charles arrived punctually at six. Sometimes he carried bags of groceries, sometimes takeout Chinese or pizza. He wore short-sleeved collared shirts in light blue or yellow, sometimes plaid, with a white undershirt that showed through; pleated slacks; and black rubber-soled shoes. He did not wear a jacket or tie. Hannah tried to guess where he was coming from, but found she could only guess where he was not coming from: he was not a lawyer or businessman, he did not work at a bank. He was probably not a doctor, either; though maybe he worked in a lab doing research like her father (who wore a pin-striped shirt and gray pants every single day). He was clearly not a plumber or construction worker: he had smooth, long-fingered hands; the half-moons of his fingernails were perfect and white. He looked like he could be a teacher, but then it didn't make sense that he would be going to work all day in the summertime. Hannah resorted to considering what sort of job the husband of Alice Lee would have, but that got her nowhere. In general, Hannah had trouble holding Alice Lee and Charles Lee as a pair in her mind; except for the first meeting, she never saw them together.

Hannah missed seeing Charles's licorice-bean eyes, as he always wore aviator sunglasses now, even inside as he unpacked food or handed Hannah her wages. When she left, he would say, "Have a good evening," and always in an adult voice, as if Hannah were not a young girl but a restaurant hostess, or one of the grocery checkout ladies. When she looked into Charles's aviator lenses, Hannah tried to pretend she was looking straight into his left eye again, but all she saw was her own warped reflection, in which her forehead appeared huge, and her eyeglasses too round.

On the one hand, Hannah was glad about not having to make conversation. She was glad, for instance, that she did not have to be driven home by Charles Lee. She'd seen a movie once on TV where the husband pulled over on the side of the road, strangled the babysitter, and dumped her in the river. The scariest part, she thought, was that they didn't show the actual strangling, only the man (who looked like a teacher) reaching toward the girl with both hands; then the camera shifted to the outside of the silver Jeep with tinted windows, which sat still and silent in the dark night.

But then again, if Charles Lee drove her home, maybe he'd take off the sunglasses and not be scary at all. Maybe she'd find a way, again, to make his shiny black eyes go wide and a little confused. Maybe that voice—that strange, familiar, inside-her-head voice—would come back, and Hannah would say things she'd never said out loud before; wonderful, interesting things she only half-knew she'd thought. Maybe, too, she'd hear that sad woodwind warmth again in Charles's replies.

Before leaving, Hannah always told Charles briefly what they'd done that afternoon, what they'd had for a snack, usually too some report on Benny's troublesome behavior. On that front, Hannah had found she had no trouble administering effective punishment: the boy hated two things above all else—silence and wearing shoes. And so Time Out meant putting on his sneakers and sitting in the Silence Chair. For his sixth birthday, Alice Lee's brother had given the boy a plastic digital watch, which he loved and wore every day. To keep him busy Hannah would set the stopwatch for two minutes. The countdown, with its racing milliseconds, at least partially absorbed him; so while he whined and pouted all throughout the lace-up of the sneakers, he kept quiet for the two-minute period. Once, Hannah had offered Veda the chance to set the watch. The girl considered seriously for a moment, brow furrowed; then she raised her eyes and shook her head. *I'll have no part of it*, she seemed to be saying, and went back to beading a bracelet.

One evening Hannah described the shoes-and-Silence-Chair procedure to Charles. The children were off washing their hands. "You're a pro at this," Charles said. He raised his sunglasses off his nose to rub his eye, then dropped them back down. "You figured it out pretty quickly."

Hannah had gone home that evening wondering what he'd meant by "it." She felt she knew even as she tried to understand. "It" had something to do with the girl's superiority, and the boy's stupidity. "It" was something she and Charles now shared, this understanding, and was something Hannah felt quite sure Alice Lee did not share, did not understand.

On the Metro ride home now, Hannah sometimes replayed the father-and-babysitter scene from the movie. She imagined herself as the babysitter and Charles as the murderer, only in her version, when he pulled over to the side of the road, Charles reached to pull her into an embrace. Once, while she was swimming backstroke at the pool, his clarinet voice came into her ear. The voice was soothing, and kind, complimenting her on her long, smooth strokes and speed.

The boy was eating lo mein with his fingers and letting the noodles hang down from his mouth. "Raaahhhrrr!" he was saying, "I am the swamp monster!" Benny rolled his eyes up almost to complete whites. Charles sighed into the refrigerator, reached for a Pabst, then closed the door extra slowly. He'd had a long day at work; the East Gate cameras at the stadium were malfunctioning again.

The boy was waiting for someone, his father or Veda, to react.

Charles turned to his son: hair like a tumbleweed on top of a cactus. Swamp monster, indeed. "We're taking you to the barber shop on Saturday."

The boy had told his mother he liked his hair this way, and she'd said fine. Later, Charles and Alice had argued over—discussed—it, and Alice told Charles that children need freedom and a sense of self-determination. They also, Charles said, need to learn how to sit still; this was the real reason, he knew, that the boy didn't like to have his hair cut. He was six years old, what did he know or care about liking his hair one way or another? You'd be surprised, Alice had said, how early it starts now. How early what starts? The importance of appearances, and self-image. Good god, Charles had said, though now he couldn't remember if he'd said it out loud or only in his head. He'd expressed it one way or another; Alice's hard silence had made that clear.

As a child, Charles himself always had short hair. His grandmother made sure of it. By the time Afros were getting taller and fuller, he'd enlisted. Only once—when Benny was a toddler just starting to walk on his own (and learning to make fists and throw tantrums), and life was becoming a constant chaos of noise and mess—Charles went two months without a haircut. "You look like Bill Withers," Alice had said, and she'd sounded pleased about it. Charles remembered her saying that, because he remembered they had sex that night—rare in those days—and Alice had shocked him by giving fellatio. Charles always sensed her semi-unwillingness to use her mouth in any sensual way—she never ate tomatoes because of the sliminess of the seeds, and she bit off bananas with her lips pulled back, teeth bared. That night, though, Charles hadn't cared. He pushed Alice to her knees. Had he pushed hard? What was "hard"? Where were his hands while she did it? Where were hers? Charles couldn't remember.

"Stop it, Benny. That's gross." Veda had spread a thin layer of pork and cabbage and was rolling her moo shu pancake into a narrow tube.

"Here," Charles said, reaching over from behind. He unrolled the pancake, dropped in another large spoonful, and re-rolled it. "You need to eat more, V. Skin and bones." He pinched Veda's upper arm playfully. She squirmed and giggled, then picked up her pancake with both hands. A strand of hair fell forward into her mouth as she got ready to take a bite; Charles hooked it with his finger and tucked it behind her ear.

On Saturday Charles took Benny to the barber. He'd been going to the shop on the corner of Georgia and Keefer Place since he was a boy. He'd known Vernon Mills for twenty-five years. In the end, this was how Charles had gotten Alice to agree: it would be a tradition, a father-son outing. Alice liked the historical notion of it, and she liked anything "special" that Charles did with the boy. As for Benny, *just like Daddy* was something to which he was generally responsive; it was how they'd potty-trained him (well, almost) at five and a half.

Vernon was not much of a talker. He let his customers do all the talking, and he listened. Charles had always liked this about Vernon—not only was he comfortable in his silence, but generous. After Nona dropped him off, young Charles would sit quietly in the chair while Vernon clipped away, sometimes humming. Usually he had a cigarette going, ashtray within reach of the chair. Charles would will himself not to cough and stare into the corners of the mirror, where he could see everyone in the shop. The other men, most of whom weren't there for haircuts or shaves, would talk, and talk. Charles didn't understand most of it, but what he perceived in the talk was that what they were saying, and what it really meant, were different things. For instance, the tone was often complaining—taxes, mayors, wives, landlords—and yet the collective feeling was one of joy and pleasure. It was something that would come back to him, and ring familiar, in small moments, years later in the Army.

Charles vaguely dreaded bringing Benny to Vernon's. He considered taking him to a different shop, where no one knew him. His friend Dennis, who he came up with (and who'd talked him into enlisting when they were seventeen and no-count), had always gone to Van's on 11th and Kenyon. But Charles had already told the boy about Vernon, and whatever lie he might concoct to fool him now would need to be elaborate. Anyway, even if the boy believed it, his mother wouldn't.

"Well, well, what have we here?" Vernon spoke in almost a whisper now, his lungs and throat worn to reeds. He'd always slouched, but the slouch had curled into a stoop. He seemed ancient, though in fact he couldn't have been much older than sixty.

"Vern," Charles said, nodding. "My son. Bennett."

"Bennett Lee, Charlie's boy. And how are you, young man?"

"Fine." Benny was pulling at the hem of his long T-shirt with both hands, twisting back and forth.

"Fine, *what*, Benny." Charles put his hand on the boy's neck and pressed with two fingers.

"Fine... thank you," Benny mumbled.

"Fine, thank you, *sir*," Charles said, and Benny looked up at him with eyes that made Charles shudder. If the boy had the words, Charles thought, if the boy were smart, he'd be saying, *You fraudulent fuck, the word "sir" has never once been uttered in our household, and you know it.*

Vernon's nephew Mike interjected then, slapping the chair opposite Vernon's. "Come right here, little man. I'll take care o' you today." Mike was a fat man, gregarious and cheeky, everything Vernon was not.

Benny plopped into Mike's chair, staring up at him with wonder. It took a moment for Charles to understand what exactly had captivated the boy. Then Benny said, "I want *those*," pointing at Mike's braids.

They were tight against his big skull, skinny rows hanging down the back of his neck and beaded at the ends. On Fat Mike the Barber, pushing forty, they were fine, they said Cool Cat; he was an exuberant born-again, he led Bible studies for prison inmates, the braids were like plainclothes. On a young boy wearing too-big T-shirts, it was a different story.

"Something tells me your pops might have something to say about that," Mike said, eyeing Charles.

Benny was quiet, his face radiant. The boy, Charles saw, had a vision of himself—one he was too young to fully understand, and yet, maybe, there was also a child's wisdom to it, something essential. *The importance of self-image*, Alice had said. Charles smiled and shook his head—not at Mike, nor at Benny, but somewhere inwardly.

"You know, why not?"

Vernon's eyes grew wide. Mike's narrowed. Charles shrugged his shoulders, which, for a blessed moment, felt looser, unburdened. Vernon shook his head too, but in his case it meant, Boy, you better know *what* you're doin'. Vernon had had the occasion to meet Alice once, at a wedding.

Benny watched all of this, eyes big and waiting.

"The boy knows what he wants," Charles said.

Benny pumped his fist into his hip. "Yessss!"

Mike called in his cousin Yvonne from the back, where sometimes her girlfriends came in for manicures and extensions. "We need reinforcements; small, strong hands," he said to Charles. Then to Yvonne, "What's your sister doing today?"

"Maureen? Nothin."

"Get her over here. So these gentlemen don't have to be here all day."

It did take some time, and while the girls prepped for Benny, Charles sat back in Vernon's chair. "While we're at it, let's shave mine, all the way down. Gimme that baby's bottom special."

Vernon shook his head again, this time laughing from the gut. "You want a shave, too?"

"Nah. Let's grow that."

Everyone set to work. There was industrious joy in the shop, all around. Mike stood back and let the girls and his uncle work. If he wasn't already, Mike would be the new boss soon. They needed to bring in more young men to stay in business, maybe this was A New Day, fathers and young sons coming in together, before they started losing the boys to the corners and all the rest.

At one point, Benny did get restless, wiggling around in the chair. Charles reached over and set the boy's stopwatch, two minutes at a time. It worked like a charm.

—<o>—

The Monolith

Eric Wagner

Some time ago, while visiting my parents in Oregon, I was leafing through their local newspaper and came to the obituaries. I'm not old enough yet to make a habit of reading obituaries, so I was about to move on when I saw one for Betty Phillips, my childhood piano teacher. She had passed away a month before in some small Maryland town, where I heard she had moved to be closer to her daughter. The news of her death had taken some time, apparently, to make its way across the country to this coast. She had been 87.

Stirred by an unexpected melancholy—it has been almost 20 years since I played the piano with any seriousness—I sat down to read. The story began, "People who knew Betty Jane Phillips talk about her as a force of nature."

*

I started taking piano lessons when I was eight years old. Like a vast majority of youthful musical conscripts, my relationship with the piano vacillated between indifferent and resentful. I had some talent but not a lot, and in any case I struggled with the rigors of consistent application. Each day I could be made to practice for precisely one half hour, muddling through scales and butchering lite ditties that were the supposed gateway drugs to more complicated works. Then the egg timer would *ding!* and I would bolt. During weekly lessons, a pack of similarly indifferent and/or resentful kids and I banged away at the upright pianos in Betty's studio for an hour or so until she sent us home.

The years passed and the other kids drifted away, drawn to the more conventional pastimes of rural life in coastal Oregon—football, hunting, fishing, whatever. I, on the other hand, kept taking lessons. This was due more to spiritual inertia than any great love for music. My most significant artistic achievement was to perform a simplified version of the theme from *Chariots of Fire* for my high school concert band, but otherwise I remained defiantly unmotivated, refusing to devote even a second more than the daily half hour. Still, by the time I was 16, I was Betty's most senior student, and in grudging acknowledgement of mutual longsuffering, she gave me a ticket to see the pianist Andre Watts in recital.

I had never been to a live piano recital. I would perform in Betty's annual student concerts, but for those I simply had to sit in front of 20 some parents, blunder my way through a Bach two- or three-part invention, and look forward to a blessedly piano-free summer. It never occurred to me that, alone, someone might play the piano in front of thousands of people for almost two hours; much less that anyone would pay to sit through such an event. But the ticket was expensive, so on the appointed night my father drove me into Portland and dropped me off in front of the Arlene Schnitzer Concert Hall.

Only after I'd gone inside the hall and found my seat did I begin to appreciate the full measure of Betty's generosity. My vantage was excellent, the seat about a third of the way back from the stage, slightly left of center in the orchestra section. I could see the keys of the massive concert grand, the shadows between them. Then the lights dimmed.

Andre Watts entered stage left. He was short but powerfully built, and after an almost perfunctory bow, he advanced on the piano as if he were about to fight it. When he sat at the bench his shoulders strained against the seams of his tuxedo jacket. He leaned forward, took a quick gathering breath, and raised his hands to begin the first piece, a rondo by Mozart. It was a welcoming introduction, glittering and impish. Watts had beautiful hands, with long, slender fingers. He danced across the keys, caressed them. Sometimes he appeared to be dusting off the keyboard, so light was his touch.

The Mozart ended, and then there was another piece, and another. Feeling heavy about the eyelids, I checked the program. The piece closing the first half was to be Beethoven's Sonata in f-minor, Op. 57, better known as the *Appassionata*.

The atmosphere in the hall became somehow heavier and more severe. Watts arranged himself, glowered at the piano, and began: a slow, descending arpeggio, deep and ominous. The figure repeated, and again, this time with what the program notes called the "fate motif," which Watts played with such menace that I shivered. Then in the highest registers, minor thirds struck sharply—cracks of lightning—and Watts's hands tumbled down in a series of broken diminished chords. The first theme returned in powerful dense chords with quieter lines interspersed, whipsawing my ear this way and that, which led to a repeating E-flat in the left hand that beat like a nervous heart as Watts's right hand leapt fretfully about. At last, in seeming summation, the principal theme returned in warm, reassuring octaves. But then the second theme burst out in a fury of sixteenth notes and the harmonies came in waves, towering up, crashing down, building, towering, crashing once more.

Watts played as if on fire. In the earlier pieces, he sometimes hummed with the music or smiled at the piano, his eyebrows dancing. Now he snarled, tossed his head, snapped his jaws. It was the most visceral art I had ever seen, and I sat, enraptured, as he brought the first movement to its end with a sequence of keening arpeggios that rocketed up and down the keyboard. Then the low growl of the first theme once more, and then silence.

Often, when a movement ends, the hall becomes a chorus of coughing and sneezing, as concertgoers give release to whatever bodily functions they have repressed for the sake of the performer. When Watts finished the first movement everyone was silent. He took a moment to compose himself before starting the second movement, a gentle theme-and-variations. This began with a quiet hymn in D-flat major, which was then syncopated, fragmented, embellished and quickened, the voices switching between the hands in seamless exchange. Where the first movement was wrath, this one was grace, but whatever reprieve it allowed was unsettled by a dark lurking energy, which roared out in the third movement that followed without pause. More than the first movement, this one was an exercise in fluid, almost frenetic pace. Watts swayed as he played, gyrating around some axis on the piano bench. His hands shot across the keys like frantic spiders. The sound grew and grew, filled all space, as the movement built to its climax: the coda.

Watts attacked it, stomping as the sonata crashed to a close. The final arpeggios cascaded down, and in a state of seeming savagery he pounded out the last chords, which blasted through the hall. So concluded, he slumped over. We stared at him, then erupted. Watts hauled himself up, bowed once, twice, thrice, and exited. We stayed for minutes more, clapping in unison—clap!-clap!-clap!-clap! The stage door closed and the lights came up. Still we stood, howling for him.

When it was time for my lesson the following week, I marched into Betty's studio and told her I wanted to learn that piece, the *Appassionata*, and also that I wanted to become the best pianist in the world. She smiled and said that it was probably too late for that. When I refused to be turned away, swearing up and down that I was prepared to do whatever it would take, she gave me a book of Hanon scale exercises and told me that was as good a place to start as any.

I went home and practiced for three hours without a break, running my hands up and down the keyboard until my knuckles bulged and my fingers felt like they were made of hard rubber. Even then I willed myself to go an hour more, Betty's parting words rattling in my mind. She had told me that I had to decide whether I wanted to be a big fish in a small pond, or a little fish in the sea.

*

Betty knew the sea and its meanings were important to me. I grew up half an hour from the Pacific, and had just started working for a local environmental group called the Haystack Rock Awareness Program in Cannon Beach. Haystack Rock is a coastal monolith more than 235 feet tall, made of volcanic basalts that are at least 10 million years old. Nearly every calendar that has anything to do with the Oregon coast features a picture of Haystack Rock somewhere, usually backlit by a glowing sunset.

As with most things having to do with natural history, the job was not glamorous. Every time a morning tide was sufficiently low— usually distressingly early—I would put on my monogrammed red anorak and drive from Astoria to the Cannon Beach City Hall. From there, my colleagues and I, a crew of three or four citizen-naturalists, would fetch a rusty municipal pickup and head down to the rock. We put out a few signs and set up a table on sawhorses, on which we laid plastic tubs filled with sand and seawater. Being the youngest of the crew, and thus the sharpest of eye and quickest of hand, I set out with a little net and bucket to collect creatures from the tide pools for display. Peering under algae, hefting barnacle-encrusted rocks, I snatched up an assortment of small shore crabs, sculpin (a type of fish), and sea stars. For the next several hours, we proffered our knowledge to whoever visited our displays, but mostly we patrolled the tide pools, intercepting people as they tried to make off with living souvenirs. We politely explained that removing organisms was illegal, and also whatever they were taking would likely die before they even got home and stink up their car, so, really, what was the point?

Yes: what was the point? For me, that question had other implications. Before the Watts concert, I enjoyed the work at Haystack well enough. I liked being outside, liked the seabirds that nested on the rock, liked all the other little critters. But in the throes of my new musical passions, I grew bitter. Every moment I was on the beach was one I was not at the piano, practicing to make up for all those lost years.

Time could crawl. Sometimes, when the sky was gray and the beach all but deserted, I would sneak off. There was a small passage on one of the large rocks in front of Haystack that I could slip through. If no one called after me, I clambered down to a little nook at the base of Haystack proper, concealed from the beach behind subsidiary pillars of rock. The route was treacherous, covered as it was with slick green algae, but the columnar basalts in the nook made a nice chair. I could settle in and watch the waves, losing myself in the white noise of their pleasing and resonant booms. I loved the nook. From the shore it was of course clear that Haystack was huge, but it could also seem oddly formless, like a cardboard cutout of a big rock. When nestled in its side, straining to see its summit, I could better appreciate its enormity.

Some distance from my nook, around the side of the rock, there was a cave. At low tides, those so rare that they occurred only every few years, one could enter it and walk a short way. Years of wave action had excavated the cave into a tunnel, but it curved such that its exit was just beyond view. In this it hinted at larger mysteries. I had heard what was on the other side, on the back of the rock: seals hauling out to bask in the sun, storm petrels bounding among the swells, an ocean unbroken all the way to Japan. But I had never seen this inaccessible world. A previous summer, during one exceptionally low tide, my younger sister and I scrambled as far as we dared until we saw a clammy haze of light. Then a wave hit the tunnel's seaward side and slopped up to our shins, and it occurred to us just where we were: underneath a massive rock, with the mighty Pacific lying in wait. We shrieked in terror and delight and scampered back.

Perhaps because of this trepidation I was largely content to sit in the nook. It was, of course, flagrantly illegal for me to be there, but I didn't care. I was an artist, or a burgeoning one. I burned with secret fires.

*

In the afternoon, once a program at Haystack ended, I would rush home to practice the piano, or to Betty's studio for a lesson. She lived in a pink rambler in a small township between Cannon Beach and Astoria called Lewis and Clark. Her music studio was detached from the house, behind the carport. She had three upright pianos and a small five-foot grand. Little plastic busts of the Great Composers presided atop the pianos— Bach, Schubert, Mozart. The studio windows looked out on fields where her neighbors ran a few cattle. Past them, Young's River was visible.

Betty was from a small town in northeastern Washington. She was a prodigy, her musical talent apparent early. She started piano lessons when she was six years old. Her first teacher, she told me once, would blindfold her as she played Bach to hone her ear, her touch. During the summer, he locked her in a church to practice for several hours at a time, to keep her focused.

She had moved to Astoria in the early 1980s with her husband, who passed away shortly thereafter. She then opened her piano studio and taught local kids according to the methods of Robert Pace, with whom she'd studied at Columbia University. Weeknights, to earn a little extra money, she played piano at a lounge on the Astoria waterfront. She dazzled the patrons with her perfect pitch, her near total recall of any song she had ever played, and her sight-reading wizardry. When time and circumstance allowed she would perform, as she put it, more seriously. Once I went to hear her play with the community band in the converted church that was Astoria's performing arts center. She strode out onto the small stage dressed in all black—at nearly six feet tall and in her early 60s, she was an imposing figure—and I watched with some amusement while the musicians struggled to keep up as she thundered through a Rachmaninoff concerto.

Faced with my newfound zeal, Betty told me that if I wanted to take the piano seriously and learn the *Appassionata* then I would first have to confront the physical limits of expression. Music was as much physiology and biology as artistry, and after years of indolence I was about to ask a lot of my hands. She took mine in hers, which were rough and enormous, and examined the tips of my fingers. "They're too soft and round," she said. "They should be flat, broad, calloused."

I redoubled my efforts with the Hanon exercises, playing until my fingers bled.

She suggested we meet earlier, at 6:30 in the morning, when the mind was fresher. As the sun crept over low hills, she told me more about the Beethoven. She did not dwell on his famous deafness, his infatuation with and eventual repudiation of Napoleon, other well-worn anecdotes. She was more interested in the idea of Beethoven as naturalist. Bach had the church, Mozart the court, Chopin the salon, but Beethoven ruled the earth and sky. His were natural affinities. Richard Goode, perhaps his finest living interpreter, had said of his works, "These extraordinary man-made things evoked in me something of the sense of wonder I had felt about animals and natural history." Just what exactly that meant was unclear to me, but Betty was sure I would figure it out. "You have an earthy technique," she said. "That's good. Beethoven is not just about transcendence. Sometimes you have to root around in the dirt."

A couple of weeks later, after much isolated toil, I brought the first movement of the *Appassionata* to a lesson and muscled my way through a very un-Watts-like rendition. Wrong notes fell thick and fast, but I felt I had captured something of the essence of the piece. When I finished, I was giddy.

Betty was inscrutable. She told me to start again, and she would stop me should the need for further instruction arise. I nodded, raised my hands, and played the first measure.

"Stop," she ordered.

I stopped.

"What do you think of when you play this?"

I considered. "I don't know," I said. "I guess a big army coming over a hill or something."

"Really?" she said. "Interesting. When I play it, I think of Death."

I blanched. Obviously I did not have the proper feeling, or was unwilling to test myself against certain metaphysical barriers. I thought for a moment, summoned up whatever capacity for audacious overstatement I had, and said, "When I play I feel like I'm talking to the gods."

Betty shook her head. "No," she said. "You aren't talking to the gods. The gods are talking through you. You are their vessel, their medium." She paused, searched for words. "You are a priest. And like a priest, if you aren't careful you mistake your slavery for power. And then you wonder why no one follows you."

I was silent. Betty had never spoken like this before. Usually she was wry, witty, insouciant. I started to understand there might be something more at stake. We were contending against more powerful forces, while outside the cows chewed their cud.

*

Spring turned to summer, and I spent more and more time with Betty in her studio. We met three mornings a week, and then I came back in the afternoons to practice on my own. At the piano, I tried to translate my bursting heart and muddled head into something that resembled musical coherence—that tricky calibration of mechanical fastidiousness and emotional release that constitutes mature performance. Slowly, and at times agonizingly, I became more adept at passages that once tormented me. Sometimes I hardly recognized what my hands were doing as my fingers rushed over the keys, following orders that did not seem to come from me. It was mesmerizing, an almost trance-like state, but also unsettling. I felt like I was being visited by a skill that would leave me the moment it detected a hint of conscious awareness, like when you fly in a dream.

The German poet Heinrich Heine wrote that when words leave off, music begins. I was finding this to be true in ways that perhaps even the poet did not intend. Once one no longer needs as much technical guidance—use the fourth finger here, play the arpeggio this way—instruction becomes more abstract. Betty's directions were like koans.

Every note you play must be a complete statement.

You should be able to end the piece on any note.

Listen with your fingers.

Your fingers should be like the roots of a flower, sinking into the keys, always seeking water.

This last one she said she paraphrased from a Maeterlinck essay, which she photocopied for me. My approach to the *Appassionata*, she felt, might benefit from some scholarship—a little less heart, a little more head. There are unities in music, she said, both within the score and outside it. She implored me not to become one those "piano-eaters" who spent eight hours a day at the piano, who saw music as life itself, rather than as one art among many others, each contributing to a conversation about life. When I looked at her in confusion—was she telling me not to practice as much?—she sent me away. It occurred to me only later that, while she had things I desperately wanted (talent, skill, knowledge), I might also have something she desired (choice, possibility, more years before me than behind).

At home, at Haystack, I devoured essays on Beethoven, on music more generally. To buttress the naturalist theme, Betty gave me Kant. There was precedent, she said. "'The moral law within us and the starry heavens above us'—Kant!!!" That scribble in one of Beethoven's notebooks is his only known reference to the philosopher, but it was enough to justify selections from *The Critique of Aesthetic Judgment*, in search, she said, of the sublime.

I was casually familiar with the idea—awe, terror, inspiring outdoor scenes, things like that. But Kant gave the sublime more of a spiritual hue than earlier philosophers, who had seen it primarily as a response to natural phenomena. He argued that it could not be found in nature alone, but rather in the relationship between nature and the mind. For him the sublime was not the soaring mountain or raging storm. It was the realization that the mind conceiving of the majesty of the mountain or the storm was both outside of and in a way superior to them. We see but cannot comprehend the fullness of what we see, and from this incapacity comes reverence. "The mind feels itself set in motion in representation of the sublime in nature," he wrote. "This movement, especially in its inception, may be compared with a vibration, i.e., with a rapidly alternating repulsion and attraction produced by one and the same Object. The point of excess for the imagination is like an abyss in which it fears to lose itself."

It was heady stuff. Having something in mind that could never be physically realized? This went to the core of my musical being. At the piano, I tried to interpret passages as one who has lost sight of the base of a monolith before he perceives its summit. Again, I wasn't entirely successful. The point, Betty said, was not to play an essay into sonata form. Don't try to recreate what made the piece astounding 200 years ago—make the piece astounding now. Refract its natural vitality through your own prism, creating newer dialogues. Like so: from Beethoven to Kant, from Kant to the rock, from the rock to the shore, to the sea around us, and back to Beethoven.

I augmented my reading with a broader if still literal-leaning eye. "The emotional force of the classical style," musicologist Charles Rosen wrote, "is clearly bound up with the contrast between dramatic tension and stability." Analogs of this tension were everywhere. At Haystack, for instance, one of the things we loved to tell people was that life in the rocky intertidal is constrained by two things: competitive prowess below, and the ability to withstand prolonged exposure to the sun above. The strongest competitors occupy the spaces closest to the water; the smaller species make due above them, subsisting on sea spray. Organisms segregate themselves precisely, the boundaries between them maintained by constant pressure and strain. From my nook I saw these clearly demarcated bands of life as the staves of a score—dotted by the occasional quarter note of a sea star—and felt the full heart-swell of interconnected being.

Beethoven's music, Rosen had written somewhere else, is full of memories and predictions. When I read that, I thought he meant the composer's own memories and predictions. I dug through his published correspondence trying to find what they might have been, but Haystack showed me alternate endings. The waves, the continuous rises and falls of the first movement of the *Appassionata* that I thrilled to—these were peaks of desperation. I was to feel the frustration of the music attempting to free itself from the tonic key, only to return to it again and again. In the deconstructed silence of the second movement, I heard a bittersweet memory of unrequited longing. The quick third movement, the one that Carl Czerny, Beethoven's most famous pupil, said should be "only rarely stormy," I heard as a cool calculus of betrayal.

Another day, I pulled a slim volume from my pocket and read that Beethoven's secretary, Anton Schindler, once asked the man himself the meaning of the *Appassionata*. "Read Shakespeare's *The Tempest*," Beethoven was said to have replied. His answer prompted some apocryphal speculation. Maybe he was joking, or maybe he had never read the play and just liked the way the title sounded. But I thought I understood, for *The Tempest*, at its heart, is about two people who find themselves marooned on a large rock.

*

Near the end of the summer, I determined I had gone as far as I could under Betty's tutelage and would be better served if I had a teacher of greater reputation. To me this seemed a natural progression—an evolution, if you will. I explained all of this to Betty as best I could and discontinued my studies with her. I found a teacher in Portland who had trained many famous pianists. She accepted me as a student, and with assured skill prepared me for the pageantry of conservatory auditions. The following spring I auditioned at several and was admitted to a prestigious music school, one I really had no business getting into. When the dean called to welcome me, I danced around like a fool. I called my new teacher and thanked her for all she had done. I called family and friends who had sweated out the wait with me. A month or so later, I ran into Betty at a grocery store and told her my excellent news. She said she was happy for me, although I thought I detected a hint of acidity in her compliment. I thanked her all the same, and then made some excuse and ran out to the parking lot. That was the last time I saw her.

*

The rest of the year passed as a blur while I prepared for music school. I practiced with a greater serenity now that my promise was externally validated. At the beach, I continued to tell people about the marvels of life in the intertidal, but my mind was usually elsewhere, and I snuck out to my nook when circumstances allowed to commune with those greater forces that were, at last, willing to grant me the audience I deserved.

In August, just before I was to leave for music school, a storm hit the beach during our program. This was not unusual. Oregon beaches are known for being windswept and cold, and even in the height of summer, rain can wash through. We waited until it was clear the storm wasn't going to let up, and then returned the creatures to their tide pools and took down our tables and signs. The truck packed, my fellow naturalists prepared to leave. But this seemed an auspicious gale, and I held back. "Go ahead," I told them as we all huddled against the truck. "I'm just parked on the street above."

I waited until they had driven out of sight, and then I went to my nook. There I stood, breathing in the sea air. The rain was fresh and warm. In a few days I would leave for the landlocked Midwest. Here was my chance to see the parts of Haystack I had always wanted to, but had been denied. The tide was not especially low—it was actually rising—but flush with daring I started past the nook, picking my way along the side of the rock. Each shuffle brought a delicious thrill of fear, but in the lee of the rock I was mostly shielded from the wind and rain, and handholds were easy to find.

Then I passed onto the backside of the rock and was at last exposed to the sea and the storm. The rain lashed my face and the red anorak was pressed flat against my chest, its loose fabric snapping violently behind me. The wind tore my breath from my nose. My foot slipped on the thick blanket of seaweed and for an instant my toes were immersed in the ocean, not deeply, but enough to give my stomach a hideous lurch. In that moment, I realized just what a terrible idea it had been to try going all the way around the rock. Everything that from the beach side had seemed fragile and small here was brutish and strange—hulking sea stars, enormous mussels, pendulous anemones that hung obscenely from the rocks. Before me the waves tossed and chopped with rebellious force. Cormorants gazed down at me blankly, while above the gulls wheeled and screamed. It was a chaos of sight and smell and sound, a chorus at once mesmerizing and terrifying, this music at the limits.

My head spun. I started to shiver, then convulse. I clung to the rock so tightly that I cut my fingers. Thin tendrils of blood leaked onto the algae. I took a deep breath to gather myself and then retreated. After many anxious moments, I made it back to the nook, and then at last I was safe on the sand. It took me several minutes to catch my breath before I could make my way unsteadily to my car. When I got in and slammed the door, I put my head against the steering wheel and closed my eyes, trying to block out the roar in my ears of waves beating ceaselessly on the rock—the pounding, and the pounding, and the pounding.

—<o>—

"A Residential Area of Portland." 1973. U.S. National Archives.

An Interview with Mitchell S. Jackson

Interviewed by Connor Guy · May 2016 · New York, NY

Mitchell S. Jackson is a writer from Portland, Oregon who now lives in Brooklyn, New York. He is the author of the acclaimed autobiographical novel *The Residue Years*, which Roxane Gay, writing for *The New York Times*, called "powerful" and "affecting," remarking that "Jackson's prose has a spoken-word cadence, the language flying off the page with percussive energy." His many awards and honors include the Whiting Award and The Ernest Gaines Award for Literary Excellence. Additionally, he has been a finalist for the PEN / Hemingway Award for debut fiction, the Hurston / Wright Legacy Award for best fiction by a writer of African descent, and the Center for Fiction's Flaherty-Dunnan First Novel Prize. He teaches at New York University and Columbia University. Earlier this year, he released a documentary about his life and his writing, also called *The Residue Years*, on *Literary Hub*.

—<o>—

Interviewer

Let's start by talking about the Northwest since we have that in common. What does it feel like, as a writer, to be a Northwesterner out here in New

York? Writers come here from all over the world, but do you feel that where you come from informs your practice or makes you stand out in a way?

Jackson

When I first moved out here, I didn't know any other writers from Portland. Well, I knew writers from Portland, but they weren't here. And so I felt alone, in a sense, but it also felt special to me, like it was an opportunity to... I knew I was always going to write about Portland, so it felt like being here gave me an opportunity to elucidate in writing some parts of Portland that hadn't been touched yet. In one sense, it kind of dampened my sense of community but then on the other hand I thought, "oh, I could really do something out here." I don't so much worry about how what I write might relate to a New York audience or an audience somewhere else. I think in writing honestly (I'm not talking strictly about facts) about the experiences I choose, it will touch someone else. Tell the truth and let people come to it. Or not.

Interviewer

Do you see yourself as a Northwest writer? A Portland writer? You speak in your documentary about "getting out"—feeling that maybe there wasn't a future for you in Portland, that you needed to come here because this is where people come to make it as a writer. Would you ever go back? Are you a New Yorker now?

Jackson

I'm *definitely* not a New Yorker now. I actually still get turned around on the trains. But more than that, I don't write about New York. Most everything that I write is grounded in Portland and home and the people I encountered while I was there. And, you know, I wrote a few essays about mentorship in New York, but... So, one of the questions that I always find myself revisiting in some way when I sit down to write is "how did I get here?" And a lot of that is examining the early stuff, before I moved to New York. Because I think that was really most influential in shaping me. So yeah, man, I don't know if I would call myself a Northwest writer, because I don't live there, but Portland is always at the heart of what I'm writing.

Interviewer

There's been a lot of change in Portland recently, and the pace of gentrification has only grown more intense as the years pass. I suspect that when most people think of Portland today, they think of the TV show *Portlandia* —hipsters, organic food, general fussiness. But that world is so far from the world we see in your novel. In what ways have you seen or experienced this divide? How does it affect Portland's overall identity as a city?

Jackson

Well, I didn't really experience that divide much while I was there. I was just reading an article today—it was actually a sociology report—and it was talking about white flight, how when black people began moving to the cities during the Great Migration, the whites who had inhabited those spaces left. And I think it's interesting that when we talk about gentrification we don't call it "white return," because that's essentially what gentrification is. That term obfuscates what's happening. When I think about Portland, I think it's really easy to get upset about what happened, but it makes sense—the industry and the commerce and all of the things that people want to do are in the heart of the city, so once they get sick and tired of driving like 75 miles to get where they want to go, they just come back for good.

But the other thing is that it's such a long plan. City planners had to know that this was going to happen in the 70s or the 80s. It's easy to think of it as a conspiracy. Because in a way it was: they had to red line and raise prices and let crime go. That seems very conspiratorial. But on the other hand, we were a part of that process, too. Like, no one put a gun to my head and said, "sell dope on this block." And my drug dealing, our drug dealing and the elements that come with make it easier for someone or something to displace us. So I feel ambivalent about it. On the one hand, I feel like we were set up for this to happen, but on the other hand we were participants in making it happen.

Interviewer

In a way, I felt like your novel *The Residue Years* offers a kind of alternative history of Portland, of the Portland you don't see on TV. You describe so many restaurants, bars, and neighborhood spots in such detail—probably beyond what has ever been written about these places before. As Portland changes because of gentrification, do you feel that one function of your work is to preserve or commemorate those places?

Jackson

Absolutely. I think I've said this before, but I want to create a record that we existed. And that existence now is being erased. Like, the area I'm talking about in the book and the documentary, it just does not exist there anymore. So without *The Residue Years* and without other stories that go back to that... like, there may be sociological records and reports, but that can only go so far... without these stories, there will be very few records of this life, and that is an experience that shaped me and a lot of the people that were around there at that time. So if I were to make a list of my goals that would be high up there. I can't think of another novel about that time and area in Portland, which makes me feel a deep responsibility to do my very best in portraying it. It's a part of our collective legacy.

Interviewer

Do you feel like fiction is uniquely set up to do that?

"Old houses, Portland, Oregon (USA)." 1967. John Atherton

Jackson

I think fiction is uniquely set up to do it in a way that doesn't feel didactic. Like, if you read a sociology report, you know you're getting information that's meant to prove a point. But fiction engages you in a way and makes you care about the people in a way that you might not if you read about the same events in an academic report. I think fiction does the work without it seeming like much work. And it opens up more space for empathy.

Interviewer

Where do you find the line between fact and fiction in a book like *The Residue Years*? The cover has "A Novel" crossed out, which I thought was a clever way to hint at its double nature. As I understand it, and as I think you've acknowledged all along, much of the novel is autobiographical. What went into your decision to write this as fiction rather than as a memoir?

Jackson

Well, when I first started writing this, I had no idea about the genre. I was in prison and I was just writing. But somewhere along the line I realized that some of the people I was talking about... wouldn't take too kindly to me writing their stories. So I figured, "well, I'd better learn some fiction really quick!" So that was really the nexus of why I went from nonfiction to fiction. But then when I learned more about fiction and when I got to a graduate writing program, I saw that fiction gave me the most leeway to get at a deeper truth than what was in the facts.

I also think that the tool belt of a fiction writer probably has the most tools in it. You could have everything that you have in poetry, everything that you have in creative nonfiction, but it's not vice versa. You could be a poet and only write lyrics in which case you wouldn't have to worry about narrative. You could be a nonfiction writer and lack a skill that's in the repertoire of the poet or fiction writer. I think fiction writers, the kind I admire, are also poets. They also have the skill set to write nonfiction. So I thought that fiction opened me up to possibilities that I wouldn't have had if I'd stuck to nonfiction.

One of the big themes that I see in your work is the idea of living in the present. There's a great line in your documentary—something along the lines of "it's important to look back to move forward." There's also a scene in the novel where one of the central characters, Grace, tells her family, "it's not who we were, it's who we are, right here." It's a beautiful idea, but you also explore how living only in the present can become dangerous, how it overlaps with the logic of addiction, with desperation. And this becomes particularly evident as things spiral out of control for Grace and her son Champ at the end of the book. How do you reckon with this dual nature of living in the present?

I think that a part of that is... Grace is saying that because, to some degree, people who have troubled histories have to live in the present because the past anchors them. They would have a really hard time navigating the world and being happy and trying to figure out how to maintain some semblance of a life if they could let go of those things. But then on the other hand it becomes like the YOLO excuse, right? Like, "I can do anything because I'm living in the moment." And I think that's really dangerous. But in both instances, I think the person has to be aware... like, it can't be an absolute. You'd have to try to recognize what element of that you need.

So if you take me, for example, how would feeling conflicted about selling drugs to people's family who I knew serve me as a 40-year-old college professor? So at a certain point, I had to let that go in order to do some work on... changing. But then, I can't now... On the other hand, so

"State Police in N East Portland." 1973. U.S. National Archives.

when I was in that world, if I made $7,000 in a night, I was like, "Oh, I'm gonna go spend five," right? So I think that's really dangerous, too. I had to figure out what is it that I need. And I don't know how people do that. I don't know how my mom navigates the world without feeling really, really down about her experiences. But I guess the people who figure that out, those are the ones who succeed, and the ones who don't...

Interviewer

So in a way, living in the present is a kind of defense mechanism.

Jackson

Yeah, like a coping mechanism, for sure.

Interviewer

What do you think it takes to get kids growing up in your old neighborhood today, kids who face the same problems you faced, interested in literature and in expressing themselves through the arts? And in what ways do you think literature and the arts can help them?

Jackson

Well, one of the ways to get them interested is to make writing and literature competitive with the arts that they're already involved with. So, I mean, most of the kids are probably listening to music, reading a lot about fashion. I think the average kid who's from where I'm from is concerned with how he looks, where he goes. And he's definitely concerned with music, because he thinks that makes him cool. So if there were some way to connect literature to those things in a way that they could recognize, I think that could be part of it.

I also think we need to have more people who look like them that are involved with writing, more role models who they can aspire to. Even inside of what we call African American lit or literature from the African diaspora—there's a wide range of different kinds of ethnicities, different kinds of writers from different backgrounds. But I feel like the guys that are from where I'm from (I'm speaking specifically about guys from my old neighborhood, which is not that neighborhood anymore), they're like... they have a really narrow sense of identity. And there are not a lot of people that fit that identity even in the group of people who are in the African diaspora, there's not a lot of people who fit that kind of template for them.

Interviewer

One concern you keep coming back to in your writing is how people project their identity to the world, particularly with words. In a scene at the barbershop, for example, the central character, Champ, gets scolded by the barbershop owner for his "smart boy vocab." And I think a big part of Champ's identity is this "smart boy vocab," his intelligence and his ability to express himself in a really sophisticated way. But Champ speaks in different registers to project different identities to different people—to his mother, to his brothers, to his girlfriend, to his friends. Why is this?

Jackson

Well, when I hear that it makes me think of the James Baldwin essay, "If Black English Isn't a Language, Then Tell Me, What Is?" He talks about the necessity of Black English, the vernacular. He's arguing that it should be recognized... but there's a line in there where he says, "If I may use Black English." So he's arguing for it and then there's a moment where he asks, "can I use it?" to the reader. And I thought, "well here is Baldwin recognizing that in some instances this language doesn't have the power that he wants it to have, even as he's arguing for it." So what does that mean? It means you have to be able to switch. Right? Any person of color who is successful has to be able to switch between the dominant language and their own—I assume that most of them would not have grown up in the dominant language—or you're screwed, I mean, you're not going to make it. So I think that's something that Champ recognizes, but what he recognizes perhaps even more than I recognized growing up is how much power there is in being able to speak the dominant group's language. How much more credible that can make you. But then also how much credibility you can lose when you speak it to your core group. Like, it's almost the worst thing you could do in some instances.

Interviewer

Well this is also related to writing, right? I wonder if another reason this question comes up in your work is because, as a writer, you're inhabiting so many different voices and perspectives. One thing that struck me about *The Residue Years* is how different the voices of your two narrators, Grace and Champ, are—but they also sound completely right and believable. How do you pull that off and how, as you see it, are language and identity tied to writing?

Jackson

Well, there are two things in the writing. There's trying to create a believable voice—that took a lot of... at least for Grace that took a lot of interviewing and listening to people. Grace is really a composite of the different women that have inhabited my life since I was little. And so I was talking to them, listening, asking questions, paying attention to their idiosyncrasies. And then, with me, Champ is like, who I would want to be. He's like Mitchell on steroids.

For the writing though, I'm consciously aware of the reader. When I sit down to write, I'm usually writing to my former self, to the twenty-two-year-old guy who's into some trouble—who's smart, but not necessarily literary. But I also know he's not the reader for fiction. I find myself feeling really compelled to speak to both of those readers in a language that they'll recognize. So really, it's the force of the readers on me, and then the force of wanting to create something authentic that kind of pushes me to those voices.

Interviewer

I was really interested in the sections where Champ speaks to the reader directly, and also the way he's always specifying who he means when he says "we"—it's always in parentheses, "(the we being me and my boys)." And that made me think about who you're addressing the book to.

Jackson

I wanted to create a chorus. I'm always looking for ways to create to chorus, to bring something back with repetition. And yes, I'm always trying to define my audience. One of my mentors, John Edgar Wideman, said that the best stories are like letters, that the readers want to feel like they're an interloper to private communication. And that's the most intimate you can get with the reader. I think when I'm talking about "we" like I'm talking out loud, I'm just allowing you to hear me. Sometimes I just speak directly to the reader. So those "we" parts are really beseeching you to join in with me, to believe me and participate. I spend a lot of time in the book, and even in my nonfiction, saying, "believe me." In some way, I'm saying "trust me, trust and believe." I do a lot of that. I want you to join in so that I feel like I have a partner in this.

Interviewer

At times I almost felt like you're addressing an outsider, someone who doesn't know where you come from and what your upbringing was like—maybe even a white reader specifically. (It may be that reading the book as a white person, I felt this more acutely.) Was this something you intended?

Jackson

Yes, that was intentional, but I don't think I'm always addressing the outsider. Sometimes, I'm addressing... Like, I remember one time in the book where Champ addresses the reader and is like, "are you tired of my pussy monologues?" That's not really addressed to any particular ethnicity or gender. It's really like a mea culpa. But I thought this is for the person who's really invested in the book at this point. It doesn't matter to me what that person looks like. I want them to feel like I pulled away some layers to just let them see.

Interviewer

Another related idea that you keep coming back to is authenticity. At one point, Champ says, "Admitted, most days I'm percents of a stone-cold fraud, but which one of us is authentic 24/7?" What drew you to this idea?

Jackson

Well, I think especially for black males, a great part of their identity is built on this sense of manhood, and so... there's this book—I don't teach it, but I used to talk about it a lot in my classroom—it's called *The Cool Pose*. It talks about how so much of a black male's identity is built on this idea of coolness, and how it's something that is both empowering but also damaging to them. Everybody wants to be a breadwinner you know, and feel educated and feel like they can take care of people. But when you can't do it, then you have to find other means of building your sense of identity and your sense of worth and I think this is why black males especially are concerned with feeling authentic in the world, because when you can't provide and you're not as educated as you'd like to be, you feel like a fraud. Right? Then they're always trying to figure out a way to say, "no, no, I'm..." No other group is as concerned with being "real." You don't hear white dudes going around saying "I'm a *real* white dude." You listen to hip-hop, in like every song—"I'm a real nigga"—they say that in every song. I'm like, "why are you so concerned with it?" But it doesn't exist elsewhere and I think that's because we've been dismissed and emasculated in such a way that... it's like a way to get back some masculinity.

Interviewer

I remember in your novel, in that same barber shop scene we were just discussing, Champ sees an old classmate who he says always puts a lot of effort into acting tough: "he plays like he's too tough for TV, a mutha-fuckin man of steel. But hold up before you knock it. That's how it is for us. How they made it... What I know is, no civilian should have to be that tough."

Jackson

Yeah, I remember that. It's like, "why can't you just be a human being? Why do you have to walk around like..." I was telling my students in class today about this study I read where they argue that trauma can change your actual DNA and be passed on to your offspring. They did a study on Holocaust survivors, and they saw that the trauma they experienced did something to their DNA, which has been passed on to their children, and in some cases it can go to your grandchildren. And I was thinking, "well, damn, obviously the Holocaust is a traumatic experience, but so was living through slavery"—so what kind of trauma was passed down through the generations? So you think about that, and then a person who lived through the trauma of reconstruction, then the trauma of the people who were terrorized under Jim Crow, which then may have been passed to my parents' generation, which could still very well be in me.

So I was telling my students about this because of this other story. I said, there was one time in Portland, I was at Irving Park, one of my favorite parks, and there was a shoot out at this basketball tournament. And when

"Interior of Union Terminal, Portland." 1974. U.S. National Archives.

I say shoot out, there were like seven or eight guys shooting, and they ran across the street and they were shooting over cars like cops and robbers. And that afternoon, during the shooting, I saw this guy—he was famous in the neighborhood because he was in the car during the first gang murder in Portland, he wasn't the shooter but he was there. All of the guys went to prison, but he was the first one that got out, and that afternoon was the first time he had been out in the public. We were all sitting out on the benches in the park, so when they started shooting everybody jumped off the bench and scattered—but not him. Like, he was so calm. He didn't jump or run. We were all hiding behind trees, and I just looked at him and thought, "why isn't he scared?" Now I think, maybe there's something in him that's made him conditioned for trauma in a way that the rest of us aren't.

Interviewer

From having lived through the trauma of being involved in the gang murder and going to prison?

Jackson

Or maybe his parents or his grandparents had experienced some kind of trauma, which was passed down, so now he's sensitized to it in a way that the average person isn't. The average person hears gunshots and is like, "I'm outta here."

Interviewer

I want to ask about the title of your novel (and the documentary): *The Residue Years*. When it shows up in the book, it's the character Mister who says it. (Champ is dealing drugs and Mister is Champ's supplier.) In this scene, he's advising Champ about how much dope to take, how much he thinks he can sell, and he says: "One or two or twenty—get all you can while you can but not a gram or a dollar more than that... You want to last, that's how you last... Most of us, if we're lucky, we see a few seconds of the high life. And the rest are the residue years." There's a lot to unpack there, but I wondered if you could talk a bit about the meaning of the title and its importance.

Jackson

Yeah, so... we're talking about a situation where people are deprived of resources. I think what the drug dealer covets even more than money is to be visible in his community. For people to recognize him. So he comes by... I remember the drug dealers would come by and, you know, give all the little kids something, and park his car in the park with all his jewelry on. He wants you to recognize that he is a success, again getting back to the idea of how he builds his manhood. But there's obviously a danger in that because then you become the target for the people who don't have that yet.

And that makes me think, there was this guy named Darren Ezel—rest in peace—who was a really slim guy. We used to call him goggles because he had really big glasses. And of the street-level drug dealers, he was the one that came up first, so he would have his Benz, he would park his car at the park, and lean on it. And everybody was like, "There go Goggles!" But they kidnapped him, took him to his apartment, to his girlfriend's apartment where they thought all his money was, and when they couldn't find it, they shot him in the nuts and said, "tell us where the money is." Well, the money wasn't there and he wouldn't tell them where it was and then they killed him. There's a consequence for being visible in the community. "Get all you can while you can but not a dollar more than that" is recognizing that there is a consequence to pay for too much wealth.

And then the line, "you only get a few minutes of the high life"—it's interesting that I had Mister say that, because Mister is a character that was based on my O.G., like the guy who really got me going selling dope. He was selling dope himself from the 80s to the early 2000s, without ever getting caught. I think he got caught in like 2006 and he got sixteen years—at the time he was fifty-something. So it's like, you had a career, you had it going thirty years... That's retirement! But you didn't stop. And so now I feel like he's in his residue years. He had more of the high life than any one drug dealer is supposed to ever get, and he still couldn't quit. He couldn't follow the advice that I put in his mouth as a character.

Interviewer

So the residue years are basically what comes after the fall?

Jackson

Yeah, it's like my uncle. I have an uncle who was like... there's a newspaper and I still have some copies (it's a defunct newspaper now) but the headline said, "Superman Goes to Prison" and the subtitle was "Oregon's Biggest Drug Dealer Gets Caught." They caught my uncle in 1982 with like $384,000 cash in his trunk. Since then he's struggled with addiction for many years. Now if you were to see him, he might ask you to borrow a few dollars. So that's the residue years.

Interviewer

There was an article that went around a few months ago about Oregon's founding as a "White Utopia."

Jackson

Yeah, I saw that!

Interviewer

The article says that "When Oregon was granted statehood in 1859, it was the only state in the Union admitted with a constitution that forbade black people from living, working, or owning property there. It was illegal for black people even to move to the state until 1926." Did you have a sense of that history, growing up there? Did it shape the way you experienced Oregon growing up there?

Jackson

Well, not in any recognizable way, because I didn't know about it at the time. But then you look back at it and it all makes sense. Like, how is it... if we were to look up the statistics now (and I haven't done it in a long time), blacks have never been more than ten percent of Oregon's population. And you're like, "well they don't have any more exclusion laws, how'd that happen?" But it's built into the DNA of the place. Remember what I was saying about how trauma can be passed down through generations? Well, you're also passing down a sense of how you want this place to look forever and ever. So now it makes sense that the population is so small... that Oregon is, in a sense, a white utopia. There's probably no better place to be white than Oregon. I don't know, maybe Vermont or Rhode Island or something.

Interviewer

At one point in the documentary, you're talking about when you were going about the process of getting your novel published, and you say, "My first impression of the publishing world was, 'that shit is not set up for me.' I wasn't represented there." You go on to talk about how you ended up in a good situation with an incredible editor and publishing team, and it seems that they really did right by your book—but in what ways did you experience publishing as a system that was not set up for you?

Jackson

Man, so, before I get to that—right now *The Guardian* is in the midst of posting the "Top 100 Nonfiction Books of All Time." So I was like, "let's see what they've got." I thought it was going to be the whole list but they've only got one through fourteen up right now. Of the fourteen, there was one book by a person of color on the list—and it was President Obama! Like, you got to be the president of the free world to get on the list if you're black? So I started thinking, "Who would be on here? Well damn, they called Baldwin the greatest nonfiction writer of all time. So how is it that not one of Baldwin's books is in the top fourteen?" It just didn't make any sense to me. But then it made absolute sense to me that this is how people build value in literature. Like, is the person who did it racist? I don't know—probably not. On the other hand, he's definitely exclusionary to think that only one person of color deserves to be included in the top fourteen. Granted, they did have a good number of women, so that's good at least.

But for me, I remember when was at the Center for Fiction dinner. It was the first time where I was in a room where I felt like the publishing industry was there. There were publishers and there were editors, and I looked around. I remember this one dude was there who I knew from somewhere else, he came over to talk to me and he was like, "Mitch, look around." And we looked around and we said, "we're the only ones here." And it was like hundreds of people. I was like, "whoa, that shit is crazy."

Interviewer

I just wanted to ask briefly about your new book. Without giving too much away, can you say a little about it?

Jackson

Sure. It's called *Survival Math*—it's narrative nonfiction and it takes the story of my family and uses it to explore their issues, which I try to connect to the historical context. So for example, my mother's addiction, which I've already written about—I try to connect that to the War on Drugs. One of my uncles is on death row so I'll take that and connect it to issues

"Portland, Oregon at night." 1974. John Atherton.

with the criminal justice system. I had a father who was a pimp, which I talked about in the documentary; I'll take that and connect it to the history of prostitution. It's asking the same question that I ask of myself, but for them. How did we get here?

Wow, that sounds fascinating—are you still working on it?

Man, yeah. I'm supposed to turn it in this summer.

Ah! Well, good luck. To close: I saw you a couple of weeks ago speaking at an event for the PEN Prison Writing program. I know this is something you care a lot about. Can you talk a little about the importance of that?

Well, it's for the same reason that I'm writing to that version of myself. I don't think that those guys see enough people that they recognize themselves in who are serious about writing. Like, there's guys out there, who will go to prison, get out, write a hood story, make some money. That's not what I'm talking about, I'm talking about really living the writing life, being involved, being a literary citizen, and reading the good work and trying to do the good work. I think that until there are more people doing this who they can recognize, we're going to be hurting, right?

I don't think that there's much more respected in the world than a serious writer. And when you say someone who's a serious writer, what you really mean is that they're a serious thinker. You could be a celebrated athlete, but the people in the boardroom see you as a celebrated athlete and a commodity to sell some products to someone, and they don't necessarily respect your intellect. And that's something that writing makes the reader and the audience do, is respect that person's mind. So I want to bring that to them. If we could create a couple more Dwayne Betts or NathanMcCalls, then... great.

The Widower Muse

Michael Upchurch

Tone is everything. Content is nothing.

Sage Bentham—"the poet of impersonality," as one critic called him, or "the fastidious seer of the motor-vehicle interior," according to another—stumbled onto his style early on, in his twenties, and scarcely veered from it in the dozen years that followed, painting after painting. The smooth acrylic surfaces, the sturdy utilitarian shapes, the absence of any human presence—these were the hallmarks of a Bentham canvas.

And the focus of his work?

As the critic said: Vehicle interiors.

Car interiors, bus interiors, train interiors. Ferry interiors, airplane interiors or any enclosed space that, by electro-mechanical or combustion-engine means, transported people from one location to another… the distinguishing trait of these images being that the people these vehicles were designed to carry were nowhere to be seen.

He painted the vacant insides of truckers' cabs, lit by the metronome of highway halogen lamps. He painted unpopulated ship interiors and showed in them a special fondness for the shallow white curves and repeated wooden doorways of maritime corridors. He once, as a joke, did a completely empty San Francisco cable car plunging down the steepest block of Powell Street without even a driver at the stick—his most fanciful flight of imagination, perhaps, since even in January you hardly ever see a cable car less than half-full with tourists.

Each painting involved obtaining a certain access, for Sage always shot photographs (his "field research") before getting his brushes out. Obtaining access wasn't difficult early on when it was just a question of gaining entry to friends' cars. (Sage had never learned to drive.) The beat-up Volkswagen of his first boyfriend Galen, during his last year of high school in Yakima, may have been what got his "Vehicles of Transport" series started. But after he moved to Seattle and his ambitions grew, access became more complicated. And promiscuity, to which he was inclined anyway, became more useful.

He would haunt every gay bar on Capitol Hill and a host of other watering holes to get what he was after. If he needed a trucker, he would find a trucker ("Vehicle of Transport No. 124" through "Vehicle of Transport No. 137"). If he needed a yachtsman from Shilshole, he would find a yachtsman from Shilshole ("Vehicle of Transport No. 202" through "Vehicle of Transport No. 209").

Other conquests included a Gray Line double-decker bus tour guide ("Vehicle of Transport No. 78" through "Vehicle of Transport No. 87") and a pre-9/11 airline baggage-checker (one of few instances where Sage strayed from empty passenger vehicles, the focus here being an empty luggage-conveyor belt). A bisexual Boeing engineer had granted him access to the spanking new interior of the 777 when it was first coming off the assembly line, but hadn't managed to smuggle him aboard the vessel's first test flight. An Alaskan ferry steward he knew had arranged to sneak him down into the engine room, but was never able to get him up into the bridge. The never-visited bridge and the 777 in flight were both lasting regrets for Sage—but he held firm against painting any vehicle interior he hadn't studied himself. Imagination, he liked to say, can only take you so far; what really counts is hard work and careful observation.

Throughout his twenties Sage remained the sprinter, the charmer, the trickster, the dancer, the sprite, dropping in on everyone's parties and going through boyfriend after boyfriend. The moment he hit thirty—it was as if a clock had struck somewhere—he settled down.

He still went dancing and he still put on his usual sartorial display—scarlet bow-tie, chartreuse sportsjacket, candy-colored saddle shoes. But now he had an anchor in the corner: Wally. His sex-for-access antics simmered down. He had enough of a reputation by now to gain legitimate entry to most of the venues he was after without making himself part of the bargain. Also—it was almost as though he hadn't realized this was possible before—he started painting a number of "vehicles" that any member of the public could enter for the price of a ticket—the elevators up and down the Space Needle, the trolley car along the waterfront, any number of buses easing their way through our newly-built bus tunnel (a "vehicle of transport" within a "corridor of transport" producing an interior-within-an-interior perspective).

The resulting paintings, it has to be said, were brilliant: endlessly inventive within their constraint, full of tension and play and illusory surfaces. Some might call this photorealism, Richard Estes-style, but it was photorealism with some kind of warp or distortion running through it. And those qualities became especially pronounced with the advent of Wally—Wally who, in turn, came as a surprise to all of us. It made sense for Sage to be hooked up with *someone*. But why, we asked ourselves, this guy?

Of course we never thought to reverse the question—to ask what Wally saw in Sage, since we felt that was obvious. Each of us had slept with him at some stage of the game... or, if not "slept," then "cuddled"—for there was nothing Sage liked better than "a good cuddle." By the time Dan walked out on him, there were dozens of men around town who would have scooped him up (he was just the right size for scooping), and it wouldn't have surprised me if he'd landed an older, wealthier man who wanted to be his patron. He still had the diminutive, elfin looks to serve as someone's "trophy prodigy." At the same time he had crushes of his own—he was obsessed from a distance for years, for instance, with an usher at

Benaroya Hall whose dark shaggy eyebrows, leonine eyes, gray flowing beard and upturned mustache promoted ecstasies in him.

"My Scottish sea dog," Sage called him. Or alternately: "My Scottish sea-god."

The man did look a bit like Neptune, but as far as I know the two never got anything going with each other.

Sage had only a passing interest in rock stars or movie actors. Instead he preferred to find his glamour more locally and in the flesh, as he had with his Symphony usher.

"Such a beautiful Asian teller," he would say, "at Wells Fargo—Westlake branch. You should see him. Nice smile. So graceful, so slender. But slender-strong, you know?"

Or: "I keep winding up at Safeway at night. Such a cute cashier there. His name is Sven—"

Or simply: "I wonder who invented waiters…"

Making it sound as though they, in particular, were a special miracle that had, with intentional effort, deigned to visit his world.

Certainly there was no shortage of dashing, handsome waiters in Seattle—which just made Wally all the more inexplicable.

I argued with Sage about Wally.

"Look," I said, "you've got a name now. You could walk up to almost anyone and say 'Want to be my boyfriend?' and they'd probably say yes. Or you could tell them you want to draw them. Use that as your opening. See where it goes."

"But I don't do people."

This was true now, but it hadn't always been true.

"What about at Cornish?"

"That was just at school."

"But you could always go back to it. How about your Symphony usher?"

Sage pursed his lips in distaste: "I only want to admire. I don't want to exploit."

Here was a fastidious side of him that always took me by surprise. He was willing to use himself to any reckless degree necessary if it was for a painting he wanted to do—but he couldn't ask the same of other people.

"I'm a soldier of art," he'd explain sardonically. "But they're just civilians. They don't deserve that kind of treatment."

"But what if you *did* put some figures in the paintings? Having a model would be legitimate, then."

I knew he could do figures: beautiful sensual Sargent-like life studies. He'd done a charcoal sketch of me in class a dozen years ago—a nude he'd tossed away that I'd rescued from the garbage and treasured ever since, partly out of vanity (I knew I'd never look that good again) and partly because it was so adroitly done. Given his talents, it seemed to me he was cutting off an integral part of himself, ignoring whole avenues of possibility. But that wasn't how he saw it.

"The figures are there," he insisted of his paintings. "Especially in these new ones. Everything I know about the human body is at the heart of them. You just aren't looking hard enough."

I shrugged as though willing to concede, in theory, that this might be the case. But he could see I wasn't buying into it. And he wasn't happy about this.

"Surely you can sense there's *something* going on in them, some kind of force inhabiting them, can't you?"

This startled me. Why so desperate? The way he pleaded made me a little embarrassed for him. So I admitted that I could indeed "sense" something there—but that I wasn't at all sure what that "something" might be.

This was the truth. The paintings, to my eye, were pregnant with "off-screen" presences that made you want to lean into them and look around, wriggle through the cramped spaces they depicted to see where all the people had gone. His airliner interiors were a particularly strong instance of this: beautiful exercises in frustrations of perspective that made you want to *stand up* so you could see down the cabin-rows of seats to find someone—anyone!—who might be on board with you.

But it was all a tease, I felt. No one was there. No one had ever been there.

Sage disagreed.

"Wally is there," he said. "Since September"—the month Sage had met him—"Wally's been in every single picture."

We were in his studio. On the wall was his latest series, his usual variations on a close-knit theme—the sleeping cars on the Coast Starlight, in this case. He and Wally had gone on a train trip to Santa Barbara.

I tried. I went from one painting to another, and then back again.

But I didn't see Wally in any of them.

*

Wally… how to describe Wally?

A spreading heap of sloping flesh, ensconced in size-14 shoes to keep him standing upright.

Wally: a pale expanse of fatty face, beneath the crown of an already balding head (and he was only twenty-three!).

Wally: belly-sphere like a huge balloon, sleek and walrus-like, entirely in proportion with himself but out of scale with everything around him.

Wally was six-foot-four to Sage's five-foot-two and he weighed at least 300 pounds. He moved as if through molasses. He had the air of being simultaneously tough and fragile—like a brittle, oversized china doll. Sage, with unusual firmness, had made it clear we were not to question Wally's presence among us. He'd even said, in what we assumed was a deadpan joke, "Wally is my muse. Wally is my inspiration. So you'll just have to put up with him."

This, with Wally sitting solemn-faced beside him.

And so we did learn to put up with him. But it wasn't easy.

I remember one dinner party when the oddity of Wally's presence among us really hit home.

The setting was Sage's new house. He had, over the previous year, hit the local bigtime and was selling paintings, lots of paintings—including a whole series of empty elevator interiors—at hefty prices to some of the most prestigious collectors around town. With the proceeds he had bought a small bungalow with huge windows, perched on a terraced lot above the Burke-Gilman Trail, near Matthews Beach. From his deck you could see across Lake Washington to Kirkland and Juanita, with the Cascades—a turquoise-white wave foaming into stone—rising up behind them. It was August, it was dry, and had been dry for weeks. Bicyclists and joggers were sweating their way up and down the trail below us, while from just over the crest of the mountains, a wind-driven column-smear of smoke rose up into the atmosphere, sickly yellow at its base: a forest fire that had been burning out of control for days now near Leavenworth, forcing road closures, evacuations, preventative burns. It was strange to be sitting out on a warm evening, drinking wine, enjoying good food and catty conversation, while across the lake, somewhere in the picture-perfect mountains, an inferno was making this parched, warm, windy weather someone else's emergency. It was also strange to think there wasn't a single chance that this view—as magnificent as it was—would ever be painted by Sage. It simply didn't interest him as a subject.

But there were still odder phenomena to observe closer to hand.

Wally, for instance, who announced a propos of nothing, "Schiele had a mistress named Wally," then shut right up.

Sage, already a little drunk, leaned forward, intoned "Hear! Hear!" and waved his wineless wineglass in front of him. Wally, noticing it was empty and seeing all the bottles on the table were empty too, rose from his chair with a certain portly majesty and soft-shoed it into the kitchen to retrieve more *vino*.

In his absence the conversation swung around to the erotic hijinks of the current president—the blowjobs in the Oval Office, the besmirching of the famous blue dress, the drawn-out obfuscation as to what the meaning of "is" is.

"*Her* behavior I get entirely!" Sage exclaimed. "I'd do him myself—"

"That's one way to get into Air Force One," someone quipped.

Sage, ignoring this, repeated: "I'd do him myself, if he was that way inclined. I mean, look at him—he's a great big honey-bear of a man!"

At this we all looked in the direction of the kitchen, united in a single thought: Wally might be big, but none of us could picture him as a honey-bear. He was too pale and hairless and blimplike for that.

"But *his* behavior I don't get at all," Sage continued. "What does he see in her? She's just a chubby little Jewish girl who affects to wear a beret. And isn't she from *Ohio* or somewhere?"

Sage, an instinctively urban creature who'd been raised in irrigated farm country high on the sagebrush flats of the Columbia Plateau, had the native-born provincial's disdain for all other city-aspiring native-born provincials.

"California, actually," someone corrected him. "Beverly Hills."

"Whatever," Sage said. "I mean, even in my heyday I was more selective than that."

He talked of his "heyday" as if it had been decades ago instead of the mere year or so since he'd met Wally. And how could he talk about being "selective" when Wally was who he'd ended up with?—Wally who, arriving back on the deck from the kitchen, now had two large bottles of Cabernet clenched in his pudgy fists.

Brent, who like me had once had a thing with Sage back when we were all at Cornish, said: "I don't really care what he did, per se. But it's bad news. We're going to have to live with it for years."

"You think?" Sage inquired.

"Maybe decades."

"Oh, come on—how much more can CNN say about a blowjob? And what about the polls?"

"The polls won't matter come election time," Brent said. "It's a blot on his record. On the whole party's record."

"I heard," Sage said airily, "it was more like a series of blots. You know: one big one, and then a series of little trailing after-spurts."

"Well I wouldn't want to be in Hillary's shoes," Brent said irritably.

"Wouldn't you?" Sage asked. "She comes out smelling like a saint. *Stand By Your Man* and all that?"

"How many shoes do you think she has?" a boozy voice called out. "As many as Imelda? Or maybe only half as many?"

This was Dan, Wally's immediate predecessor with Sage.

"I'm sure it's an impressive collection," someone answered.

"And how about you, dear?" Dan said, turning to Wally. "Would *you* like to fellate the president?"

Dan had followed the same pattern we all had—thrilled at first to be Sage's boyfriend, glorying in being the beau of a minor local-arts-scene celebrity, then coming gradually to realize that living with Sage could actually be quite boring since all he ever did was paint.

True, Sage was in his element at dinner parties—but that was virtually the only time he came to life. It was as though he reserved all his peacock energies for when he was sitting at the head of the table. When you were with him on his own, he scarcely spoke. And the sex wasn't all that spectacular. Once you knew which buttons to push, the whole business was strictly routine—like his gaudy, fanciful wardrobe that consisted, one gradually came to realize, of only two or three strikingly similar outfits.

And a little like his paintings, too, which could look terrific all lined up under just the right light in a cavernous gallery in Pioneer Square. Seeing them that way lent strength to their repetitions—and repetition enhanced their strangeness, their power. But at home those same paintings could seem monotonous at times, especially given the way Sage worked on them. If he finished a canvas at 3:45 p.m. on a Friday afternoon, he would never just call it quits. Instead, he would start on another, before breaking off at his usual time of five o'clock. His joke—if it was a joke—was that he'd made his creative routine as much like a 9-to-5 office routine as possible: "I'm sure that's how Gilbert and George do it."

This was fine for the first few months. But then, after nine months, or maybe a year, the novelty wore off—as did that of the paintings themselves, when you found yourself living with them. There inevitably came a morning when you'd wake up, have some coffee, look in on Sage in his studio, stare at his latest work in progress and think to yourself: "Oh, great… another airplane interior." Or ferry lobby. Or Toyota backseat.

And you'd pack up your bags soon after that.

Another pattern also held true: that the moment Sage replaced you with someone else—and there appeared to be no shortage of willing successors—you'd immediately regret your decision and yearn to be taken back by him. Hence the dinner parties, which were often nothing but volatile gatherings of Sage's ex-lovers from the pre-Wally era, all trying to outdo one another, all contending for his attention.

What Sage—who wanted nothing more than a predictable lover to stick predictably by his side while he painted his predictable work—made of this process, I can't say. If it were me, I would have grown paranoid at being abandoned so frequently and then having all my faithless beaus hang on in my social circle for years afterward.

This particular pattern seemed to be coming to an end, however, with the advent of Wally. Wally, it appeared, was for keeps.

"No," Wally said, in poker-faced answer to Dan's bullying question about the president. "I only ever fellate Sage."

"So why did he do it?" someone else asked. "It just seems nuts. You'd think he'd be too smart to act so dumb."

Sage chipped in: "Because he could. Because he saw a chance to grab a little something extra. And he took it. Without really thinking about it."

He leaned forward, brimming wineglass in hand, and smiled hugely at us.

"Like most of *you*," he said with emphasis, his smile growing even broader: "You *know* you have—seen the chance and taken it."

He turned specifically to me: "I know damn well you have."

I didn't know which specific transgression of mine he was referring to, but I had to acknowledge, with a regretful smile, that he was right.

"We probably all have," Sage said soberly. "Except perhaps for Wally."

Dan, on a mission, cornered Wally again: "So then, what would you say to our beleaguered president if you were to meet him, once you'd made it clear you weren't going to fellate him?"

Wally, taking this in stride, sat up a little straighter, pronouncing each word in a bland robotic voice. "I suppose I would tell him: Mr. President, you eat just like everyone else. You sleep just like everyone else. You shit just like everyone else. So you have no special reason to break the rules. Because you really aren't all that different."

This was more than Wally had ever said at a single session. We were each a little stunned by it—all except for Sage, who had a small amused look on his face, such a bright, twinkling delight in his eye that you could almost hear him thinking: *That's my boy!*

Which was when it sank in for me, when I knew it for sure: Wally was permanent.

*

I had known by the end of my second year at Cornish that I didn't have what Sage had in terms of talent—and I began to turn such gifts as I was stuck with toward computer graphics, so as to find work as a commercial artist. What I realized, after getting some of the requisite late-night partying and club-going out of the way, was just how much work it took to be merely mediocre. Sage might be a bit on the facile side, the way he turned out canvas after canvas, all of them a little too instantly recognizable as his. But he was fluent and he drove his fluency in paints like a demon.

I couldn't begin to approach his output, either in quantity or quality. This made me jealous of him, of course, and then furious with myself for being jealous. I might mock him for his foibles, but never, beyond the odd sniping quibble, for his art. Even while I was still going out with him and found myself badmouthing him to friends over drinks ("The man can't even operate a washing machine!"), I would end with: "But of course he's some weird kind of genius—the closest I've ever come to it, anyway."

The odd thing was: by esteeming Sage so highly, by placing him on this pedestal, I forsook him slightly. I neglected him in the present because I was so busy imagining the rueful, mocking, laudatory things I would say about him in the future, at age sixty, seventy, eighty. I looked forward celebrating his contradictions—how he had come out of Eastern Washington sagebrush country, but had never painted that landscape. He wouldn't have dreamt of it! And yet he loved the smeary canyon-and-butte paintings, licked through with smoke and piercing flame, of James Lavadour.

"Lavadour is *amazing*," he would say, with a flutter of his eyes and a tweaking of his bright bow tie. "Mr. James Lavadour," he would intone, "is the fucking J.M.W. Turner of the Interior Northwest. No kidding."

This, about a man whose work, in most respects, was the absolute polar opposite of his own.

Sage, by contrast, was deliberately shallow—but I didn't think he would always be seen as shallow. I didn't even think of him, after a while, as a Richard Estes rip-off.

I remember one time we went up to Vancouver to see an Andy Warhol retrospective there. I'd gone out of idle interest because I liked the movies: *Trash, Flesh, Heat*. But I'd never thought much about the paintings. Silk screens of Elvis, Marilyn, Elizabeth Taylor... what was there to think? But then there were the JFK assassination paintings: the smiles in the motorcade before the gunfire; Lee Harvey Oswald pulling back in a crazy dance move as the bullet got him in the gut; Jackie as widow—in veils, with eyes downcast. And these were followed by some of the more messed-up self-portraits, the eyes a little piggish, the hair (a wig at this point?) halo-ing out of control.

Sage, in his saddle-shoes and little suit, was weeping. Sage, circling through the gallery again and again, had met his master—or one of his masters.

I, in the meantime, had caught the alluring eye of a museum guard who, on the breast of his handsome blue uniform, was wearing a button saying: "Ask Me About Andy."

I asked him all the way into the men's room—corner stall.

And wasn't much good to Sage for a few years after that.

*

A year went by, and then another year. And still we couldn't believe it—that Wally was really what Sage wanted; that Wally was here to stay.

I took Sage's quip about Wally being his muse as a joke at first—typical Sage! But then I wasn't so sure. I think I was misled by my feeling that, given the kind of work that he did, Sage had no real *need* for a muse. Plus, if he needed one, why choose Wally?

My prejudice—my "lookism," if you will—was showing here. But I couldn't help myself. Wally was a lump. Wally was a conversation flattener. When we got a new president who seemed even more problematic than the last one, and everyone started griping about him, Wally preposterously chimed in, in a way that shut us all up: "It's true. He may be a bad president. He may be a dumb president. But he's the only president we've got right now."

On a less political note, if the skies had been clouded week after week, and it seemed as though the sun would never return, Wally, as though deliberately to aggravate the situation, would take it upon himself to reassure us: "I agree. The weather is awfully gray just now. The weather has been gray for several weeks, I suppose. But the weather is often gray this time of year."

Thank you, Wally.

After the country was attacked, and the initial shock and the rallying around the flag had subsided, and it looked as though our "problematic" new president might turn out to be our worst president ever—how sunny, how heavenly, the blowjobs and bubble economy of the Clinton years looked to us now!—we couldn't help ourselves: we wanted to get Wally's take on it. We asked what he would say to Bush if he had the opportunity to meet him. But Wally would not be drawn.

"I'm not sure I'd have anything to say to this president," he answered primly. "Anymore than I had anything to say to the last."

"Come on, Wally," Dan said impatiently. "You're telling me that if you had the chance to meet Bush, one on one, you would have absolutely nothing to ask the man? Nothing to tell him?"

Wally, seeing he had been cornered again, straightened up, inflated himself with his usual bland, resigned dignity, and answered: "Well I suppose, if I was forced to, I would tell him the exact same thing I would have told his predecessor."

"Which was—?"

We were enjoying this. We were getting a kick out of it. We were eager to serve as Wally's chorus, in a way. And sure enough he came through for us.

"'Mister President,' I would say. 'You eat just like everyone else. You sleep just like everyone else. You shit just like everyone else...'"

And so on.

We couldn't help ourselves. As Wally continued with this litany of bodily functions, we all joined in him on the refrain—"Just like everyone else!"—which made him smile cautiously and hopefully. Was he perhaps being included? Had he finally been accepted by the circle of men around him?

No, definitely not.

In fact, after this episode it was agreed upon by all of us that Wally wasn't human, that Wally was animatronic. And this did, on some level, make a certain sense. After all, Sage—in his work, in his wardrobe, in his personal routines—had done his best to approximate a robotic regularity of habit, an utter steadiness of regimen. And maybe only someone like Wally could fit so seamlessly, so frictionlessly, into a life so strictly regulated.

Besides, we had to remind ourselves, Sage had never ditched a lover. He'd never had the opportunity! We had all been too quick for him.

So maybe he didn't know how to pull out of an affair?

Or maybe his allegiance to Wally was merely a symptom of his hankering after the predictable and the practical. He needed someone dependable in his life who could change a lightbulb, cook a meal, fix the lawnmower when it broke. I had no doubt that Wally knew how to do all these things and that Sage didn't know how to do any of them. He had no clue how to run and maintain a household, anymore than he knew how to drive a car. So it had to be Wally who kept Sage's pretty new bungalow (and its decks!) in such smart shape, who kept the whole business from leaking, rotting and falling down.

But was that enough? It might be devotion of a sort, but could it really be called love? Then again, why was I, who mostly just acted on impulse, concerned whether it was love or not? Maybe Wally was a compromise Sage was willing to make, for the sake of having some stability in his life. Maybe Wally, for Sage, was a This-Will-Do.

I had heard Sage use this phrase a number of times before—as a feeble plea for me not to leave him ("But don't you see? This will do"); as an update on his latest boyfriend who perhaps wasn't thrilling but was pleasant enough company ("Oh, you know how it is—this will do"); or as a description of a teaching arrangement he'd taken on or a piece of gallery business ("I agree, it's not perfect—but it will do").

Brent and Alessandro, before they had found their destiny in each other, had been in This-Will-Do relationships with Sage, first one of them, then the other. Dan and Sage had been such a flailing, operatic duo that This-Will-Do didn't really apply to them—it was more like "What the hell are we doing together?" But at either extremity of connection, whether placid or turbulent, none of us had ever been decreed Sage's "muse" that we knew of. And even though "This will do" had become an endlessly repeated joke within our circle, applied to all sorts of situations in all sorts of ways, I never once heard Sage use it in reference to Wally. In fact, I suspected, he wouldn't have dreamt of it.

This bothered me. This bothered me so much and for so long, I'm afraid, that on the one rare opportunity I had to spirit Sage away from Wally so as to interrogate him, I went for it. It was a Saturday. Wally, who'd been with Sage now for about three years, was en route to North Dakota to visit his ailing 96-year-old grandmother. (Neither Wally's apparent devotion to his ancient relative nor his family's evident longevity boded well to me, hinting as they did at Wally's continued presence in our lives—if we were all still around by then—until circa 2073.) I persuaded Sage to go on a walk with me, for old time's sake. Sage only worked Monday through Friday. He never painted on the weekend, not even when he was left on his own.

But it still took some doing to talk him into leaving the house.

"Wally might call," he fretted. "He said he would."

"But he doesn't get to Minot till ten, right?"

Wally, with an eccentricity that rather warmed me to him, wasn't flying but taking the train to North Dakota—an interesting choice. Or maybe it was the only economical way of getting there.

Sage's other objection was that he'd been thinking of going on a ferryboat ride. He had been on countless ferryboat rides. He had taken countless photographs of ferry-boat interiors. And he had painted countless images of them, in one "Vehicle of Transport" after another. Why he needed to go on yet another ferryboat ride was a little unclear to me. But after putting some strong pressure on him—I explained that I didn't have time to go all the way to Bainbridge or Bremerton and back—I was able to steer him into taking an hour's stroll with me along the lake.

Steep lanes led the way down. Bicyclists hissed along the Burke-Gilman Trail, shouting "On your left!" to dawdling pedestrians. Water-front houses with docks lined the lakefront. Sage, with his sharp features and colorful saddle shoes, his bow tie and shimmering sportsjacket, made his usual striking contrast to the company he was keeping: the Lycra-clad joggers and roller-bladers around us, the denim-clad dogwalkers and stroller-pushers. As we turned down the path that led to the beach, people stared at him and then at me, as if to see if I was aware that I was keeping company with a fashion lunatic. I stared defiantly back at them.

We found a bench and looked out, past the lifeguard and swimmers and ducks, at the lake. We talked about this and that. There was a small exhibition of his work at the Frye that was coming up—a big deal!—and he also mentioned a future project he had in mind: the possibility of doing a "vehicle interior" of a motorcycle. Was there any way, he wondered aloud, of capturing in paint the sensation one had, when riding pillion on the back of a Harley, of being "enclosed" in wind and noise and light? (When, I wondered, had Sage ever ridden pillion on the back of someone's Harley?)

And then we alighted, as I'd intended to all along, on the subject of Wally.

Sage fretted at the amount of time that Wally was spending with his grandmother in Minot: "I don't like him being gone so long." He worried whether, upon Wally's return the next week, he, Sage, would have remembered to buy all the favorite grocery items that he, Wally, liked to eat. He'd already made several trips by bus up to Lake City.

All this fretting seemed a little ridiculous to me, and before I could stop myself I said with open skepticism, "So how long do you think this thing with Wally is going to last? Another year? Maybe two?"

Sage looked at me in shock.

"Wally is forever," he said.

"Wally is *forever*?"

The words sounded so ridiculous that I couldn't help but echo them.

"Yes, he is," Sage insisted.

"So Wally is really 'it,' then?"

Sage looked at me with a pitying smile: "Wally is my muse. I thought I told you."

He fluttered a hand against his heart as he said this, like a swoon-prone Southern belle, tiny but headstrong, who'd corralled her man.

Dressed in his parody of male drag, he was still the preening peacock, still the delicate flower. And with his Gallic good looks—deep back in his east-of-the-mountains ancestry on his mother's side were fur-trapping métis merchant-traders who'd built a series of forts along the Columbia— he retained the élan to carry the whole show off.

I wanted to puncture this line he was giving me. I wanted to show him how deluded he was. And I must have been feeling reckless because I turned our conversation to his work.

"But you're all about technique," I said. "It's the technique that makes the paintings what they are."

He looked at me warily, not quite sure where I was going with this.

"And it's an amazing technique," I continued. "I'll grant you that. But it's not like it's the product of inspiration from on high, is it? I mean, it's not the kind of thing you need a muse for."

Here I thought to myself, but did not say aloud, that even the dogged way he went about painting his paintings—on a strictly unvarying schedule, with not a lick of work done on the weekend, not even a sketch, because weekends, and also national holidays, were designated "time off"—merely went to show how very little "muses" and "inspiration" had to do with all the pieces he kept churning out.

To my surprise he took no offense at my comment on his lack of need for a "muse." I almost had the feeling that if I'd gone ahead and said what I'd been thinking about the markedly uninspirational nature of his weekdays-on, weekends-off painting routine, he wouldn't have taken offense at that either.

"You don't understand," he said mildly, then got up and resumed strolling. I followed him.

Out on the lake, motorboats buzzed and, between their foamy wakes, sailboats slanted precariously. We took in the spectacle of the pleasure-boats, floatplanes and the opposite forested shore. And then Sage asked me: "Have you even *looked* at the paintings lately? The ones I've done since Wally?"

I felt guilty here. I couldn't really say I had "looked." It would have been more accurate to say I had glanced at them. But how could I admit to this?

"Of course I've looked," I said.

"And?"

"I guess I wondered what you had to do to get free access to the Smith Tower elevator car when it was empty."

Sage turned away from me. And I panicked. I feared I was about to lose him altogether. I had failed him as a lover a dozen years ago at Cornish and now I was in danger, through my own deliberate sabotage, of losing him as a friend, in spite of the fact that I admired him. And I *did* admire him, admired his work, knew it had a hold on me, even if I sometimes disparaged it. For some reason it was the subject matter, not the work itself, that was a stumbling block for me. Never mind that collectors were now paying thousands for it; and never mind that there were lots of other painters I loved without giving a hoot, one way or the other, what their particular subject matter was.

I was even willing to admit that there were millions of vehicle interiors out there in the world and that no one had ever studied them with quite the intensity Sage had. But how could you spend your whole life painting nothing but vehicle interiors? What about the view from this beachside park, or the view from his house overlooking the lake? It drove me a little crazy that it would never cross Sage's mind to paint these panoramas—or to paint Wally, for that matter, if he loved him so much.

At the same time I had to concede that the very fact that he *didn't* paint these views, *didn't* paint Wally, seemed to speak well of him; seemed to suggest a certain integrity to his actions or lack of action… although what the rationale or source of that integrity was, apart from a certain stubbornness of focus, I couldn't begin to say.

And here I'll confess: I never, even after his death, got to the bottom of it—never came close to answering the question "Why vehicle interiors?"

But this is skipping ahead. Right there, by the lakeshore as we walked it, I was stuck more on what Sage thought was happening in the paintings he'd done since Wally.

"I'm sorry," I finally said. "I just don't get it. Tell me what you're driving at."

He gave me a look so different from his usual playful-sardonic mien that I didn't quite know what to make of it. If I hadn't known him better, I would have said there was "mystical fire," or some other long-outmoded sentiment, shining in his eyes.

"Wally's in every one of them," he said.

"You mean you've painted him in somewhere, like 'Where's Waldo?'"

"No, I haven't painted him in. But he's there, if you look. You can *feel* him."

This was getting a little too woo-woo for me. "Subliminal presence" wasn't a concept I could readily associate with the massive Wally. But Sage persisted with it.

"These new ones," he said, "they're good. They're the best I've done so far. They have a tension. They have a certain spirit to them: Wally's spirit. You could say they're a sort of shrine to him."

"A shrine," I repeated.

"Yes."

"A shrine to Wally-the-Muse," I proposed.

"Yes, exactly," Sage replied, as though taking me seriously, as though he thought I'd finally gotten it.

But I hadn't gotten it.

Well," I said at length, "whatever else he's done, he's certainly bumped up your asking price."

And that was as far as I got. That was as much as he would tolerate.

We turned back from the beach, faced away from the lake-and-mountain view, started up the hillside lanes that led to his house.

As we walked, we said nothing. But I noticed with curiosity, if not quite alarm, that Sage who'd never been much of an athlete—he was the runt of his family, with six or seven older brothers all twice his size and quadruple his strength—scarcely had the breath to say anything anyway. In spite of his charming youthful get-up—boyish cowlick, optimistic tie—he looked strangely worn out, defeated. And in my paranoia I grew cer-tain that this look of his, this drained expression of defeat, was strictly emotional in nature rather than physical, that it stemmed directly from what I'd just said to him.

I haven't just discouraged him, I thought. I've crushed him! Either that, or I've given him conclusive proof that mine is not the sort of world that he or anyone with his talents would ever want to live in.

By the time we were in sight of his house, he was so pale I had to ask if he was all right.

"I just need to sit for a second," he said—and plopped right down by the roadside. "I always get tired coming back up."

He was sitting in a bed of dead and dusty leaves. But he didn't seem to notice this. His action made no sense to me. He was so tidy, so dapper in appearance. How could he be this tired? How could he bear to get his clothes dirty?

"The house is right there," I pointed out.

"In a second," he panted.

And then, after some minutes on the ground there, he lifted his small self up and made his labored way to his own front entrance.

He didn't invite me in. He didn't even say goodbye, really—just looked at me from his threshold, like a brightly costumed sparrow.

"I should check," he said. "Maybe Wally called."

And then he gently closed the door on me.

*

Sage died—not that day, not that week, and not before Wally got back from North Dakota. But by the end of that month. His heart. He'd had a problem with his heart, and none of us—not his friends, not his doctor, not even Wally—had been smart enough to guess it. He was only thirty-three. Instead of being an early-career retrospective, the show at the Frye became an accidental memorial. And I didn't just "glance" this time—I *looked.*

I looked as I'd never looked before.

And I saw.

Sage was right. There had been a leap.

Between "Vehicle of Transport No. 468" (a Toyota Camry interior) and "Vehicle of Transport No. 469" (another Toyota Camry interior) there had been an ascent into a higher tier of accomplishment, difficult to describe in words but obvious to any eye. The paintings were precisely dated, not just with the month and year, but with start dates and finish dates and even, on some of them, the time of day completed. Three years ago, at the age of thirty and within a week or two of meeting Wally, Sage had entered his "late period." And he'd been intensely conscious of it.

I was no longer a painter. I couldn't have explained to anyone the technical details involved, beyond his long-ago switch from cotton canvas to linen as soon as he could afford it. But that had been well before Wally; that didn't explain the leap. I'd scarcely spent any time with Sage in his studio in recent years, so I could only guess at what specifics—what brushes, what brush-strokes, what particular mix of paints—had been put into action to make this leap take place. All I knew was that the pre-Wally canvases, as clever and inventive and accomplished as they were, came across as mere ingenious exercises, whereas the post-Wally paintings, even when they depicted exactly the same subject matter (that Toyota interior, three sequential escalators at Pacific Place, the lower car deck of the ferry *Wenatchee*), soared. They had almost an element of protest to them, as though Sage were insisting, "This *is* beautiful, this *is* important, I *can* do something with this—something that's not just clever." There was a deliberate imbalance to the later paintings' composition that charged them with energy. There was a vivifying tint to their colors that drew you into them with an almost three-dimensional effect. I was sure that if he were still alive Sage could have told me exactly which artists he'd "ripped off" to achieve this effect—he knew his Italian Renaissance and Dutch Golden Age inside out. And he could have told me, too, why in his hands these borrowed effects of reflection and counter-reflection, of mirroring glass and burnished surface, were working so well together. For Sage was nothing if not an intelligent analyst—of both his own paintings and anyone else's. He took pride in what his paintings had accomplished, almost as though they were his children and had done what they'd done all by themselves. Although I suppose, going by our last long conversation on that walk along the lake, he wouldn't have said it was the paintings that had done it this time. He would have given credit to his "muse": Wally.

Wally was at the opening, of course, and I felt a little sorry for him. He was having to bridge a strange and painful gap, accepting both condolences and congratulations—condolences on Sage's loss, congratulations on the incredible show.

I got distracted picturing *myself* in Wally's position, bravely enduring my bereavement even as I savored, with pride, my feat in having brought out the best in Sage in his final years—not just the best of his talents, but of his personality. For Sage had been a little less manic, a little more thoughtful and serene in these last few years, hadn't he? Or had that just been fatigue... a symptom, perhaps, of his undiagnosed heart condition?

Whatever the case, I envisaged myself in Wally's place, smiling and emotional, tearful but ecstatic, ready to explain or reminisce about Sage to all the world—especially to any reporters who happened to be in the room.

You can see how desperately I wanted to play the role of widower, and how well I thought I would do at it. But the part wasn't mine. It belonged to Wally.

Turning toward him, I expected to see small arias of display-worthy sentiment playing over his pudgy features. I expected to see him hugging people and shaking his head at the sadness of it all, then spreading his arms out at all the paintings around us, at this legacy, to exalt in what a marvelous visual world Sage had left for us to dwell in...

Wally was doing none of these things. He may have been heart-broken. He may have been traumatized, anguished, in collapse. But not a jot of this showed in his face. He was, in fact, so completely inexpressive that, as usual, there was no real telling what he was feeling.

Wally, when I looked at him, simply stood there. Wally, when I studied him, blinked back at me. Wally inertly accepted the comments and compliments and condolences given him, but gave so little back that it occurred to me to wonder, as I studied him, whether he might not be a victim of fetal alcohol syndrome or some other similar ailment. There was something *that* damaged, *that* curtailed, about his whole emotional-cognitive apparatus. How could Sage have loved this lump? Or was being a "muse" not necessarily the same thing as being loved?

I took another turn around the exhibit, examined a Cessna interior Sage had done in his twenties, a yacht's below-decks furnishings, a night-trucker's cab where you could almost taste the blowjob Sage had traded for the view from behind the wheel. These early paintings had plenty to offer too, but they were flashy, they were showy, they were almost snide comments on the world—whereas each of the post-Wally paintings was a whole world unto itself. And as such they were haunting, endlessly viewable and capable of triggering obsessions: Sage's obsessions.

Even when he wasn't actively at work on a painting, Sage was pre-occupied by it, more attentive to it than he was to any of the people or events unfolding around him. He would try to put a pleasant face on this, especially at dinner parties or gallery openings. But it was always the painting that counted for him, that was uppermost on his mind, not the fuss of openings or review coverage.

So perhaps it made sense for him to have a boyfriend who was also devoid of fuss?

I remembered when Sage first introduced me to Wally and I asked—as soon as was practical—what on earth the attraction was.

He lifted his head dreamily, paused to think, then said, "Well, he's always punctual, that's one thing. He's always so precise! You can count on him being where he says he's going to be, exactly when he said he would get there."

"But anyone can do that," I objected.

Sage shook his head sadly: "Maybe you're right. Maybe they can. But hardly anyone ever does. And if it's someone coming to see you—someone who says he'll be there to meet you when he said he would—"

His smile grew so wide he couldn't finish his sentence. Instead he just shrugged his shoulders as though in disbelief at his luck, as though recounting the most romantic episode in his life.

"It's erotic!" he insisted. "Punctuality is an erotic quality. It shows you really like a person."

I was about to disagree with this, when he laughingly me cut off.

"I mean, look at *you*," he said. "You could never make it anywhere on time."

Which made it clear I didn't have a leg to stand on.

*

In the absence of Sage, in the *wake* of Sage (for that was what it felt like—as though we were all bobbing corks on an ocean, still in agitated motion from the mighty vessel that had passed us by), what we were left with was... Wally.

Along with what paintings we had, and we all had a few, Wally became our central "connection" to Sage, our way of prolonging our sense of contact with the man we'd loved so inadequately.

But we didn't quite know how to act upon that contact, how to put it into effect.

It was partly a question of scale, it seemed. Wally was so preposterously tall. Wally was so outrageously wide. Wally was of such incredible heft—a sort of shifting junior manatee, gliding from room to room—that it was awkward to know what to do with him. And what was there left of Sage in Wally? The more we regretted our own personal histories with Sage, the more we tried to find out. It was almost as though we thought of Wally as a shrine now, a shrine containing Sage—just as Sage's last paintings were a shrine containing Wally.

Shrine or no shrine, Wally was an enigma—and a labyrinth. And there was, we concluded, only one way to find your way through a labyrinth. You had to enter it.

Dan was the first to act. He got a jump-start on the process; we hadn't developed any strategy at this point. His bedding of Wally was more a spur-of-the-moment kind of thing.

But once it happened, we fell quite easily into seeing Dan as our "advance man," our initial explorer on a quest that was, by its very nature, improbable if not impossible—to find out what it was about Wally that had taken Sage's art to another level; to uncover what Wally had been able to give Sage that none of the rest of us could give him; to see what Wally had seen in Sage that all of the rest of us had seen inadequately or incompletely. Going even deeper than that, we wanted to find, in the presence and tone of Wally, whatever remained in the world of the tone and presence of Sage.

It was a few weeks before Dan reported back to us on what had happened—those details he could bear to go into, anyway.

Wally, of course, had stayed on in the Matthews Beach house on its hillside ledge overlooking the lake, with its side-garden flowerbeds, its little deck and patio, its two tinkling fountains. He squatted there like some beast of legend, to guard Sage Bentham's legacy. The house itself, as I said, was modest. It was the setting that made the place what it was. And, again in a shallow way, it was the setting that we sometimes missed. Since Sage had died, the dinner parties had come to an end and we felt as though we were in exile from one of our favorite aeries in the city.

This naturally made us want to pump Dan for all the information he could give us.

"It must be pretty grim over there," I suggested.

"It is," he confirmed, "but partly because it's not."

"I guess it's just weird being alone there with Wally."

"Wally—" he began. "Wally—" he said again. "I'm not... sure," he finally stammered out, "where things stand exactly... between me and Wally."

"What does that mean?" Brent asked.

Wally, these last few months, had been busy, Dan said. There was a ton of material to archive—not just the records related to the more than five-hundred "Vehicles of Transport" Sage had painted, but the dozens of photographs he'd taken for each of them, plus the preliminary sketches he'd done for some of the more elaborate compositions. There was also a surprisingly large shelf of videotapes dating from Wally's arrival in Sage's life and perhaps containing vital clues to Sage's modus operandi, about which Wally remained resolutely uninformative. (It seemed typical of Sage that he'd never bothered updating from VHS to digital.) Dan had tried but hadn't found the opportunity simply to grab those tapes and go—so he had stayed and offered to help.

There was, in fact, still a lot to do, and Dan went back several weekends in a row to help Wally do it. Sage, in his twenties, had been erratic if not downright cavalier about keeping any kind of photographic trace of his completed paintings. There were some black plastic trays of slides at the bottom of a jumbled closet, but they were unlabeled and in no discernible order. The bills of sale and gallery statements were likewise a mess. Wally was taking it upon himself to document all of Sage's career—going back at least as far as his first "Vehicle of Transport"—but this involved tracking down the present owners of the paintings, some of whom were difficult to locate.

Wally went about this in a businesslike manner. But Dan, on his third weekend there had been overwhelmed by the sense that these remnants, these fragments, these paintings, sketches and photographs were all that was left of Sage. And he just couldn't stand the feeling of loss. Without quite knowing what he was doing, he "fell into" Wally—the way a small desperate boy might fall into his father, hoping to bury himself there, hoping to lose himself in a grown man's strength.

"You didn't!" I said.

"I did," said Dan.

"You couldn't have."

"It happened."

"But what did Wally do?"

"Wally said: 'Oh'—"

"Wally said, 'Oh'?"

"—and then he just sort of went with it."

"You mean the two of you really *did* it together?"

They had, he said—Wally as inscrutably as always; Dan partly faking it, putting more drama, more sense of occasion into this seduction than he really felt... but desperately wanting something from it too. Maybe absolution from his sins against Sage?

"And?" I asked.

"Nothing," he answered.

"What do you mean: 'Nothing'?"

"I can't—I can't do it—I just can't go through with it again," he said. "I told him I'd be back to help organize. But I can't. It's like a funeral over there. It's like this endless, brutal funeral where everyone keeps missing the point, mimicking the same old emotions."

"But it was only Wally and you."

"I know, I know, but it's like they keep on looking at you—all those photographs, all those paintings. And the sketches too. It's like there's people in them now. People I never saw before. And you can't tell whether Wally sees them or not."

"Dan—"

"Look, I know it sounds crazy. But I can't. I just can't. I fucked it up with Sage. I don't want to fuck it up with Wally."

Dan had never given Wally's feelings a second thought in his life. So why now? This was such a surprising turn of events, and so utterly unlike Dan, that we left the situation alone for a while. None of us contacted

Wally. What did we have to say to him anyway? Wally, on his own, had never mattered. He had interested us only insofar as he related to Sage. It had always been Sage we were there for—even if, as lovers, we'd never been able to stick by him. And we would, I think, have left the whole thing alone, would have let it heal itself the way that any loss, with passing time, heals itself, rubs itself dim—if it weren't for Dan's mention of that VHS archive.

Had Sage, in the Wally Era, undergone a change of direction and moved from canvas to magnetic tape?

Had he, in his very last phase, attempted to become a video-artist?

That would be genuinely shocking, if it were the case, and there seemed only one way to find out—by "infiltrating" Wally again, by getting as close to him as possible.

This time we had a little more discussion about it beforehand. We considered, as we hadn't considered with Dan's spontaneous forays, what might be the wisest strategy to take. And finally we agreed that Brent and Alessandro should be the next to try.

They took their challenge gradually, approaching it as a team. First they invited Wally for dinner to their apartment on First Hill. Then they went with him to a show at the 5th Avenue Theatre, and I met them there. They weren't small men, but seated on either side of Wally they looked dinky. They looked, in fact, like two debauched children symmetrically flanking an enormous maternal figure who, able to impose her will on them through her sheer physical presence, had no trouble keeping them in line.

Wally as fertility goddess?

Maybe I should have taken this fanciful thought more seriously than I did at the time.

One evening at the Matthews Beach house, when Wally reciprocated their dinner invitation and all three had imbibed sufficient to drink, things careened into the carnal and they steered Wally into the bedroom where they attempted to have some sort of congress with him. Again, at this move, Wally said, "Oh."

Neither Sandro nor Brent could remember much of what happened after that.

"I guess we overdid it," Brent said.

"I have-a bruises in a place I never have no bruises before," Alessandro said in his lilting Italian accent.

He lifted his shirt to show us.

"And what about the tapes?" I asked.

"We never even get close to them," said Sandro.

"He didn't give us any time," Brent added. "He wouldn't let us."

Had I seen where this was leading? At what point did I become aware that I was next in line?

I phoned Wally up, asked how he was doing.

He said he was doing well.

I asked if he would like to go for dinner sometime, mentioned a new place that had opened on Capitol Hill, called simply "Food"—which seemed both monosyllabic enough to be trendy and straightforward enough to be in synch with Wally's appetites.

We went there. We talked about Sage. We somehow talked about Sage without saying all that much about him.

Wally, for instance, mentioned going with Sage to Tacoma to the Museum of Glass there.

"It's not really made of glass," he explained. "But it has a lot of glass in it."

I told him, as gently as I could, that I was aware of this. Then I asked him what Sage had had to say about the exhibits there.

"Sage said he could never have worked in glass. He said he didn't see how anyone could."

This didn't seem to be getting us very far.

Then Wally and I went to see the new Altman, because—"Sage always went to see the new Altman."

We went. We sat. We watched. But at the end of the show, I couldn't tell whether Wally had liked the movie or not. I only knew that I hadn't.

I asked Wally what Sage had thought of Altman.

"Sage said some Altmans were good and some Altmans were bad. But even with the bad Altmans—"

"—he's the only Altman we have right now," I finished the sentence for him.

His eyes met mine in the mildest surprise: "Yes, that's exactly right."

I thought: This isn't getting us any further than Sage's reported opinions on the futility of glass art. But apparently our Altman date was a great success. Wally seemed to think so anyway. He apparently viewed it as a breakthrough of sorts, an initial step on our mutual path toward friendship.

"I so enjoyed talking about Altman with you. Would you like to come back to the house for a drink?"

This was it. This was my chance. I'd been handed my point of entry.

It was a clear and chilly autumn night. As we traced the lamp-lit path to the house, I could hear the wind making trees sway softly and branches rustle. From the deck out back, the houses of Kirkland and Juanita on the opposite shore were a twinkling band of lights. A yellowish moon, a *Halloween* moon, had risen from behind the Cascade Range and was shedding a pale, buttery path across the water.

Inside, Sage's final series of paintings was lined up along the wall: "Vehicles of Transport No. 527" through "Vehicles of Transport No. 534." All were roughly the same size, and each explored a different angle of playfully constrained subject matter: an empty Metro bus interior. First there was the view up the bus's entry stairs, facing the fare booth and driver's seat (with no driver in it). Then came the view down the aisle past the wheelchair spaces and seats reserved for the elderly (with no elderly or disabled in them). Then along to the "prize seats," as I thought of them, on the rise above the tires, with their higher vantage point—but again no occupants. And finally some longer shots down the length of the bus, from front to back, from back to front, with not a soul to be seen in them.

Yet you could almost hear the electric whine of the bus on its over-head trolley wires, the cellphone conversations of the passengers, and the tumbling of coins into the fare box.

Wally brought out some red wine and glasses. I emptied half the bottle. Wally brought out some crackers and cheeses. I ate most of these, then drank more wine. I stood in front of the first bus painting, imagined climbing up those steps to where a driver ought to be and no driver ever was. And then I found myself falling into Wally.

Wally said, "Oh."

It didn't take us long to make the move to the bedroom. I felt like a minuscule mountain climber, rappelling up a shallow but strangely challenging peak. I couldn't get my bearings; I didn't know where I was. I only knew that Wally's head was looming up ahead of me somewhere at the summit.

I had never been on an expanse so pale and wide. I assumed that, beneath me, Wally's penis must be hiding and I felt it only polite to try to search for it—and search for Sage inside it. But then I grew distracted, felt I was adrift on some vast and sacred carnal cloud, and let myself give in to its pleasures. That is, I gave in to my own pleasure, straddling Wally and coaxing my spasm of seed onto his skin—a skin as ripply and rolling as swells upon the ocean. Wally again said, "Oh," while making no apparent move to secure his own orgasmic release.

I had not found Sage in Wally—just as I'd never found a persuasive reason for Wally to be with Sage. But the advantage I had just taken of Wally apparently disconcerted him. Within thirty seconds after I was finished, he slid out from under me and said, "I think I have to take a bath now."

If this was what had happened with the others, if they'd even made it this far, they hadn't mentioned it. Wally withdrew behind the bathroom door, and I heard him turn the faucets on full. Given his size, I thought it was bound to be a very long bath. First he would have to fill the tub. Then he would have to lower himself into it. Finally there would be the even more cumbersome process of lifting himself out.

I knew the house well. I'd had a good account of where the videotapes were from Dan and Brent and Alessandro. And there had been plenty of times when I'd helped technology-impaired Sage operate his VCR.

I found the tapes. I turned on the machine. I popped in a cassette. I adjusted the tracking. I fast forwarded through some "snow" until I found what I was after.

There on the tape, like two genies trapped in a bottle, were Wally and Sage—naked, but not doing what you might expect two naked consenting adult homosexuals to do, especially not two who were videotaping themselves.

Sage was merely painting—and stood in Wally's embrace.

That is, Sage was in the foreground with a canvas propped in front of him and a palette of paints at his side… while Wally, cloud-like, loomed from behind him.

Sage was working on the picture I'd just looked at, of the rubber-matted stairsteps with their black cushiony grooves and, above them, the apparatus of the fare-box with its dollar-swallowing box and its glass cage for coins. Beyond them was the brown vinyl bus-driver's seat with no driver in it—while behind Sage stood Wally, half holding, half caressing him, administering to him a kind of "cuddle" I hadn't seen or heard about before.

It had been a while since I'd glimpsed Sage naked and I'd forgotten how beautiful he was—a sort of delicate, aging boy-man, with his slender hips, narrow waist, sinewy arms and comical patch of fur at the center of his chest. In this barely moving image—Sage always worked calmly, his brushstrokes anything but dramatic—he held the spot-light, shone in televised miniature.

Wally, behind him, was enormous. Wally, with his large pale arms, was an edifice that swayed. And Wally, with his wandering hands, played a sacred energy up and down Sage's torso, finding his straining cock and touching it, setting it lightly bobbing into motion, then withdrawing again, as Sage went on painting.

And all the while he whispered something into Sage's ear.

I couldn't quite hear what it was.

Quickly I checked at the bathroom door to see what progress Wally's bath was making. After hearing some reassuring noises from the tub—walrus splashes, manatee wallowings—I rushed back to the VCR and turned up the whisperings loud enough to catch them.

In the fondest of cadences Wally was murmuring to his lover: "You shit just like everyone else. You fuck just like everyone else. You eat and drink and pick your nose, you pee and burp, you walk and get tired, you lick and taste and come—just like everyone else."

Sage's cock seemed only to get harder upon hearing this. And his brushwork just got more fastidious.

I punched out the tape, put in another, which after moving through more static snapped into focus.

There the two of them were again, in the same state of undress, in the same state of sexual excitement—on Sage's part, anyway. The way the camera was positioned made it difficult to say what, exactly, was going on with Wally. Only this time the words coming out of Wally's mouth were: "It may not be a perfect Bentham. It may not even be a good Bentham. But it's the only Bentham we've got right now…"

I was getting my clue here—and it gave me no real clue at all.

I wasn't just getting my clue. I was getting my revelation! And still it gave me nothing.

Were these "late" paintings more alive than the earlier ones because they were angry reactions to Wally's words? Or were they more alive because Sage found painting in Wally's whispering embrace such a blissful and comforting experience?

Was Wally, by heaping the same ego-flattening remarks on his lover that he had heaped on our two most recent presidents, telling Sage he was as great as any president could be? Or was this whole routine a deliberate provocation, calculated to incite Sage and spur him on with his remarkable work?

Whatever it was, it wasn't anything I could ever have come up with—not in a million years. And while I knew what Sage had repeatedly insisted—"Wally is my muse... Wally is my *inspiration*"—I still wasn't sure of the truth.

All I knew was that I'd gone about as far as any of us in Sage's surviving circle of friends had been able to go. And I couldn't see taking this any further.

I found my jacket. I dug out my car keys. I tiptoed toward the door.

As I let myself out into the side garden I could smell wood fires burning nearby, putting their stamp on the moldy scents of autumn. I took a moment to inhale this smell. I also turned to absorb this one last glimpse of the lake I was ever likely to get from this particular angle—the moonlit water, the lights on the opposite shore—because it seemed hardly likely I'd return here again.

And then, I admit, I hesitated.

Somewhere in the midst of my confusion I was countered with a moment of temptation.

What if Wally had it in his power to raise my commercial hackwork to the level of fine craft? What if, through contact with Wally, I could come up with something wor-thy, something that might actually endure for a while?

I wasn't thinking of masterpieces. All I had in mind was work that might put me at or near the lowest rungs of what Sage, in his earliest days, had managed.

But no... it still wouldn't be worth it.

Before Wally could emerge from his bath—clean and huge and purified, ready to let me make further claim on him—I got out of there.

—◦—

Don't Worry

Anca Szilágyi

Johnny's teaching math in the fall and we're on our honeymoon. Venice, Rome, Paris, Amsterdam. A whole month. Sexy sexy cities for sexy sexy times. I planned most of it. He got Amsterdam.

Here we are at the Rijksmuseum and it's too late, 5 pm, closed. We couldn't sleep at all the night before, our first night in Amsterdam, the last leg of our trip: Airbnb sheets stained yellow, bed narrow, EuroVision blaring next door; and in the silences, inexplicable pounding, scraping sound of metal on metal, someone sobbing, a halting sort of sob, loud like they were pressing their mouth to the wall, then quieter and quieter, a wandering away.

"Oh well," says Johnny. "Coffee shop?"

We bumble on to the first one we find, Reefer Madness, and sit down in the back, an herby haze to smooth over life's wrinkles.

"This is nice," I offer, relieved at least, to not be milling about yet another big museum. I lean back and exhale luxuriously. "Our honeymoon should be relaxing, after all."

Johnny's eyes go soft—melted butter, olive oil. Satisfied I'm not mad about the Rijks, I think.

We step out into the early evening.

"I'm famished."

Johnny nods.

"I've got just the place. I've been waiting all month for it."

Off Leidensplein, the Times Square of Amsterdam: a smoky restaurant.

"Ribs?"

"The best in Europe."

"But are ribs Dutch?"

Johnny shrugs, runs his large hand through his hair. It's so thick it stands upright, makes me want to jump on his back and muss it up.

"What's Dutch anyway? Potato? Cheese?" He sweeps his arm in a grand gesture and says with a relishing sneer, "*Herring?*" His eyes glitter. I snatch his arms down, hug him until he says ouch.

We each opt for the smoked ribs and a baked potato and the waiter eyes us with a twinkle, must think we're fools. Heaping platters, fit for four. Four Americans, in fact, so make that eight. We rub our hands together. The salt is marvelous. The grease coats our lips, cheeks, fingers. Smack, suck. Tear strips of meat off the bone.

Eat your salad, I almost say, but it's just our honeymoon. Why nag?

Our bellies swell and groan.

"Wish I'd worn a sundress." I'd let my gut hang. I feel it spill over my low rise jeans. Little beer-meat baby.

The weed-food coma spreads open my mind. Like there are big wide gaps, like the spaces in a video game. Leap to the platforms with red-capped mushrooms to make thoughts go *ba-BLING*.

"Well, we should see *something* of Amsterdam," I say. Almost stamp my feet.

"Like what? The Red Light?"

My mind rifles.

"Anne Frank. That's the one. Everyone goes."

"Well," he says, and I can see him tamping down an eye roll. "This way north, then cut west." He's memorized the map. Good boy.

"Is it even open?"

His fingers smudge oil in the pages of the guidebook. "'Til 10. Golly!"

We grab hands. He leads the way.

The streets get busier and drunkier. Bunch of handsome scruffies sit on a dirty white couch on a broken terrace overlooking a canal, guzzling beer. Opera's playing in their house, big windows open to the world. Like they're looking to be looked at. Like Abercrombie models debauched. Nasty pretty frat boys on a gap year. One of them one day will murder a hooker. You can just tell.

Here come the sex shows. Pics of slick naked bodies in all variations of thrust. Johnny nudges me.

"How about it?"

"Well. If they're short."

There's nothing to them. Acrobatics to a techno beat. Change positions when the rhythm shifts. In out twist thrust boom boom boom boom. I yawn.

Outside, red bulbs switch on and curtains open. A skinny brunette sidles close to the glass. Little blue bruise on her arm. Blonds with boob jobs. Half of them slump on stools, scrolling through phones. Race car red or hot pink and studded with rhinestones. A fat one chugs a Red Bull. An older, larger lady, eyes lined real dark, looks askance, worried. And one, real cut, dances with her head down, silky hair hiding her face. The only one smiling is at an open door, talking up a prospect.

Johnny lets out a rib burp and laughs.

"C'mon, we did a show, now this. How about it?"

"No way!"

"But we're already here."

Impish smile.

"Should've got me a bigger diamond for that."

His bear paw of a hand swipes at me, gentle like a cub. Snakes his arm around my neck, gives me a noogie.

The line at Anne Frank Huis is short but slow. My stomach's still tight with pork. My mind still full of plastic boobies and pink silicone coochie coos. Nubbed vibrators.

At the admission desk, Johnny gets real serious, puts on his teacher face. But his eyes are still glazed. The security guard shines a light inside my purse. A sex dancer sneers up at us from a flyer and I zip it real quick with a sheepish grin. Security guard just chucks his chin. Move along.

We shuffle through a short film and empty rooms. Not much to see. Here's where they snapped a wedding photo. A woman named Miep (Meep). A woman named not Beep or Boop but Bep.

We wait for the crowd to trickle up steep, narrow stairs.

"You're in *The Twilight Zone*," Johnny whispers, breath all herb and wood smoke. "That episode where you have to choose to be one of two kinds of people. Except the choices are now Meep and Bep. How do you choose? *How?*"

I knock his head with the heel of my hand. Upstairs, more empty rooms. Except their toilet's there, behind Plexiglas. It's actually pretty, blue flowers on porcelain, like fine china. In the next room, the wall's collaged with Anne's favorites: movie stars and kittens. She named her diary Kitty.

Then there's the pictures of the piles. Naked bodies. Gristly rib bones come to mind. My stomach gurgles, mad about all the churning fat inside. We pull on our sober faces. The next room moves real slow. I can't see over shoulders. I wait. Johnny shimmies forward, darts ahead, a reconnaissance mission, darts back.

"C'mon," he's saying, pulling on my hand. "It's just papers."

Anne's dad is on a video. I had no idea he survived. He's saying something about being surprised by her diary, how you never really know your children.

We're outside again, the air cooler. What a relief. Imagine the heat of those cattle cars. The thirst and stink. "I need a drink," Johnny says. There's an unsteadiness behind his face now. He runs his hand through his hair again and it looks even crazier.

We find a chill pub by a canal. You can always find a pub by a canal. That's nice. The old sidewalk is tilted. We order two gins. Waiter looks peeved. Bunch of stupid whacked out tourists.

"Johnny," I say, fiddling my drink.

There's a nasty look, but he wipes off that face with a Justin Bieber smile.

A long-legged brunette bicycles slowly toward us. She's dreamy, indifferent, her straight hair so long it drapes over her small, buoyant breasts. Her chemise is gauzy, her blue shorts real short and real blue, twilight blue, her skin golden. She rides upright, posture perfect, earbuds in, and as she passes she's singing off-key, blasé, "You don't love me like I love you." I think this is perfect this is the perfect moment and there's the sound of something dropping. Italian dude at the next table dropped his steak knife on the cobble stones. A cruiser of red-faced blond bros glides by behind him on the canal, they're shout-singing Bob Marley, "Don't Worry," but with a military drum and martial beat, and the Italian guy, the Italian guy, he reaches for his knife and tumbles forward off his chair into the street.

—◇—

"Amanita muscaria, two views of a mushroom. Hillsboro, Oregon."
1910. The Field Museum Library.

"Begin and End with a Landscape in Peril": an Interview with Alexis M. Smith

Interviewed by Sharma Shields · September 2016

Alexis M. Smith was born and raised in the Pacific Northwest. Her debut novel, *Glaciers* was a finalist for the Ken Kesey Award for Fiction and a World Book Night 2013 selection. In 2015, she received a grant from the Regional Arts & Culture Council and a fellowship from the Oregon Arts Commission. She holds an MFA from Goddard College. Her latest novel, *Marrow Island*, has been called "transporting" (*Vanity Fair*), "weird and glorious" (*BookRiot*), and "intoxicating" (*The New York Times Book Review*). She currently lives with her wife and son in Portland, Oregon.

Sharma Shields holds an MFA from the University of Montana. Author of the novel *The Sasquatch Hunter's Almanac* and the short story collection *Favorite Monster*, her work has appeared in such literary journals as *Slice*, *Electric Lit*, *Kenyon Review* and *Iowa Review*. A contributing editor to *Moss*, she has garnered numerous awards, including the Washington State Book Award. Shields has worked in independent bookstores and public libraries throughout Washington State and now lives in Spokane with her husband and children.

—<o>—

Interviewer

Reading *Marrow Island*, which has been described by many as an "eco-thriller," I was instantly struck by your impressive range as a writer. *Glaciers* and *Marrow Island* are very different books, structurally speaking. Can you describe how you tackled those differences?

Smith

I think the first, biggest difference—and the one I was most conscious of as I wrote *Marrow Island*—was the more complicated plot in the second book. Glaciers hardly had a plot, and it wasn't meant to; it was always more meditation than story. With that postcard motif in *Glaciers*, I could begin almost anywhere and drop in details of the landscape as casually as a traveler. *Marrow Island* had so much more story that I wasn't sure where to begin, plotwise. Have you ever gone out for a hike and not been able to find the trailhead? It was like that at first. But landscape has always been my entry to storytelling, from very early days in Alaska, so that gave me a framework: begin and end with a landscape in peril.

But I also needed to have a more specific idea of how the story would end before I could begin. This was true for both books, but especially for *Marrow Island*. The two different landscapes in that book offered different possibilities for the story, and that, ultimately, saved my ass in terms of plot. I think this could have been a really soggy story, but the Malheur landscape—and the Palouse!—introduced different energies.

Interviewer

In *Marrow Island*, a colony attempts to rehabilitate an island destroyed by environmental disaster. The narrator, Lucy, knows this place intimately: It's also the island where her father disappeared. Were there similar historical instances of civil—or uncivil—disobedience that helped guide the details here?

Smith

One of the big events of my early twenties was the WTO protests in Seattle. I marched with the Lesbian Avengers one day (we were very popular with the Teamsters, who were marching right in front of us), with the Sisters of the Holy Names another evening. I saw Vandana Shiva speak on the environment and poverty, and Michael Moore speak on politics. Friends were gassed. A childhood friend was the spokes-person for a group of protestors squatting in a building downtown; I had accompanied her to lectures before the protests and was pretty sure my home phone was tapped. It was an experience in civil disobedience and social justice that I'm not sure I will have every again: a coming together of so many disparate groups to oppose the consolidation of global power by and for the wealthy. I'm not sure that it did anything to stop what was coming (global markets crashing; the poor getting poorer; global warming; the sixth extinction), but it was a formative experience and I'm sure that it influenced *Marrow Island*.

Interviewer

You made an interesting choice in *Marrow Island* regarding time. An important element of the plot is a fictional disastrous earthquake—the "big one" that everyone is waiting for, which in the world of your book has already occurred long ago, circa 1993. The protagonist, Lucie Bowen, narrates from 2016, so she's functioning in a world parallel to our own. I think many authors using a plot element like this would have launched the story into the future. I like that you avoided the futurism trope: After all, our planet is in imminent danger, not in the future but now. What made you decide to choose the time line that you did?

Smith

I love that you call it a parallel world, because that's how I thought about it. I don't know much about quantum physics, but I like how multiple universe theories are the perfect model for what we as fiction-writers do. How different or similar from our reality are the realities we're creating?

I thought about projecting into the future but it felt wrong. For one: I love science fiction, but I feel like I'd be a shit sci-fi writer. I don't care so much about imagining future technologies or political systems. I wanted to tell a story about people you could know, trying their best to deal with how we're fucking up in the here and now, but with different set pieces.

Interviewer

What inspired the earthquake?

Smith

Those of us who grew up west of the Cascades have been living with the idea of "the Big One" for most of our lives. When I was in high school in Seattle in the early 1990's, we had earthquake drills and emergency kits at school. My mom left the Northwest for New Mexico fifteen years ago after the Nisqually Quake—she had lived through the massive Good Friday Quake of 1964 as a child in Alaska (my father did as well)—and she just didn't want to live with the possibility of another one. I have pretty intense anxiety about disasters myself, and I think that's where the quake in *Marrow Island* came from—I wanted to imagine my way through a big earthquake. I interviewed my Grandma Betty about her memories of the Alaska quake, and letters from my Grandma Margie to her mother in Washington informed a lot of my description of what it was like during and after the quake on the islands. Setting it in the past allowed me to present a vision of survival—like the one my grandmothers and parents described, and as much as that was an artistic choice, I think there was definitely some therapeutic value for me, too.

"Storm clouds over James Island." 1963.
University of Washington Libraries.

Mushrooms are also a really significant part of this book—I don't want to give too much away by saying how, but there is a thin line between their ability to heal and their ability to kill, and in one gorgeously written scene, the latter proves to be more merciful. Tell me about the mushrooms, the metaphors they carry, the research you clearly undertook in learning about them, how you spun them into a flesh-like character. The mushroom kiss scene, I should add, is one of the most powerful scenes I've read in a very long time. (Gives me goosebumps even now. I won't say any more than that.)

Smith

Yes, I think the title for this book could have been *The Shrooms*. But that totally would not have made it past the publicity team. (My editor, Jenna Johnson, on the other hand, is a mushroom fanatic, so she might have approved.)

As for the significance of the mushrooms, my readers (and my friends) are smarter than I am. It wasn't until late in the book that I had a clue what I was saying metaphorically with the mushrooms. Life and death and decay are certainly on the surface here, but what you describe as "the thin line between their ability to heal and their ability to kill"—I was working that out the whole time I was writing, though it seems so obvious when people say it back to me, now. I researched quite a bit— reading and interviewing people and learning to identify mushrooms— and when you get so close to the actual thing, you can forget that in your story they're going to operate on more than the literal level. Which is fine—premeditated symbolism doesn't always shake out the way you want it to—but after I figured it out, in revisions, I struggled a bit with how to let the symbolism come through. It can feel like you're smacking your readers upside the head with it, when you're writing it. So, yes: the mushrooms are the key signifier in the story. And I'll let readers figure out what the signified is...

That was one of the more fanciful scenes—along with the mushroom kiss scene. I loved writing it.

Interviewer

This reminds me of another book I love in which mushrooms allow both life and death, Shirley Jackson's *We Have Always Lived in the Castle*. Who are you reading right now? Did any books specifically inspire or serve as guides for this novel? I know you and I have discussed in the past how we both gravitate toward reading women writers almost exclusively...

Smith

I love *I Have Always Lived in the Castle*, as you know. I, like many writers I know, have chosen spirit guides (and probably a few unchosen, who influence us despite our best efforts to ignore them). We cycle through them, so as not to exhaust them and ourselves, I think. *Glaciers* was very Jean Rhys, Virginia Woolf, James Baldwin. *Marrow Island* was mostly Margaret Atwood (yes, I know she's still alive). The book I'm brewing now is Jackson, Barbara Comyns, Sylvia Townsend Warner, Zora Neale Hurston.

Interviewer

So much of *Marrow Island* is about recapturing time and place and relationship. Lucie thinks of her father, who died during the quake, but even more deeply she thinks of Katie, her best friend from child-hood. You write very beautifully about the attractions girls have for one another, as friends and as sexual beings, and the longing between the two women to regain their relationship's foothold. I thought of Elena Ferrante as I read, the Neapolitan novels. I wonder if Katie and Lucie's relationship was your starting point in the book? Or did their friendship come to you as you wrote? It feels beautifully organic to the story.

Smith

Katie and Lucie's relationship was there from the beginning, and I thought a lot about whether their romance would be the central one of the novel, but it didn't work for a story about disasters. Their relationship is very much the kind of intense relationship young women have—and have been having for millennia, I suspect—when they're becoming women together. Becoming a woman is a process of sheer panic meeting utter despair (the earthquake can be read as a metaphor for sexual awakening/onset of menses). We officially become sexual objects at the same time we are able to become mothers. It's a ridiculous mindfuck. And the only way to navigate it is with other women (a former nun leading the Colony wasn't a happenstance detail, either), though as you said of mushrooms earlier, the ones who are most likely to heal us are also the ones who know exactly how to hurt us the most. I don't want to give too much plot away, but it felt right that Katie and Lucie's re-lationship should be a ghost story.

Interviewer

Finally, I want to ask something related to the Inland Northwest, where I live. Being from Spokane, I loved this passage when Sister Janet comments on the strangeness of the phrase "Inland Empire," "The mountains, the rivers, the Palouse, all the way down to the Columbia. It doesn't feel right. Using a word like empire in this day and age. As if we could ever own any of this. It owns us." Can you tell me a little bit about your experience with the Sisters of the Holy Names of Jesus and Mary? And with the Inland Northwest?

Smith

I went to a school in Seattle run by the Sisters of the Holy Names, who have a Provincial House (which is sort of like a regional headquarters)

"Comb Tooth mushroom plant specimens growing on tree bark, displayed on a table." 1910. The Field Museum Library.

in Spokane. One summer a group of my classmates and I went on a pilgrimage to the Provincial House to spend some time with the sisters there—many of them elderly and retired from their posts out in the world (many of them were teachers; they're a teaching order). As a non-Catholic, my experience of Catholicism through the Sisters of the Holy Names was one of women living in community with each other, with education and social justice (in the name of Jesus, of course) as their missions.

I was the only outspoken feminist and openly gay, but I was nurtured in their community. You can see the influence here on the story, I'm sure. The sisters in Marrow Island are more fanciful than the sisters I met at the Holy Names provincial house (they are not all named some variation of "Rose," obviously, that's an inside joke, of sorts)—and obviously Sister J is entirely made up. One thing that I wished I had been able to better express in Marrow Island in general—and there was a moment in the very last revision in which I tried to add a paragraph, but my editor nixed it as a panic-add—was that the presence of the Church, like the Colony, was another expression of the imperialist instinct of white people, whose intentions may be good or not, but whose mere presence tends to obliterate the existing culture and/or ecosystem. In my research on the San Juans I came across stories of missionaries marrying young Coast Salish women as cultural/economic transactions. And stories about Coast Salish children being removed from their families and shipped off to boarding schools in Spokane. We now know the enormity of this practice, and its legacy on the land and the indigenous people here. Sister J's "empire" comment came somewhat in response to this. They called themselves Marrow Colony, and in that way, they might as well have been the lost villagers of Roanoke.

Interviewer

Can you comment on your experience as a writer in the Northwest? Apart from its clear influence on the landscape in your novels, how has living in the Northwest, with its writers, its readers, influenced your writing life?

Being a regional writer isn't something I set out to do, but I'm proud to be one (if that's what I am after only two books) especially at a time when the Northwest is seeing a population boom of writers and creative types from other parts of the country who maybe don't relate to the history of the place, are still learning about the geography, or the geology, or the plants and wildlife (or don't care—that happens, too). Portland has become such a polished, urbane place, full of great writers, yes, but, I feel like a rare beast here, writing about the Northwest landscape as a living, breathing thing. Regionalism doesn't seem to appeal to as many readers as cosmopolitan dramas, or even domestic ones, for which place is just a set piece.

I'll admit to being grumpy about this. Some foreign publishers called *Marrow Island* "too American," which just baffled me. How are natural disasters and climate change "too American"? I think they meant "too regional" in its setting. Emily Carr, the Canadian artist and writer, painted some of the most incredible landscapes of her time, but she's not known like, say, Georgia O'Keefe. Why? Is it because the Northwest is still being "discovered"? I'm of two minds about this: I relish being a rare beast and knowing the lesser-known places and plants and writers (like Carr, and M. Wylie Blanchet, whose book *The Curve of Time* is my favorite memoir ever written); but I also can't stand the idea of regional writers as purveyors of novelties. Our landscapes may be strange—and they are dramatically variable from one mile to the next—but the stories that run through them are universal. I want to hoard the secrets of the Northwest, but I can't help myself—they're all I want to write about—therefore, I want them to be taken seriously.

—<o>—

The Jimmy Report

Tiffany Midge

Thursday, May 7, 2004. 11:00 AM. Bellingham, WA.

I pass by the front counter and spot him in the back, climbing out from beneath a sizeable pile of clothes. He's wearing dark blue, polyester pants from a deceased WWII veteran's closet. The pants have some sort of multi-colored dashes woven into the fabric that look like moth infestation. They're obviously too big for him, so he belts them with an orange scarf. The shirt is ordinary and coordinated with his pants.

Jimmy owns and operates Blue Moon Vintage Clothing, housed in a proverbial bulwark near the waterfront in the old town section of Bellingham. I happen to catch him on a good day. He says he's feeling good because he just received a windfall—the aforementioned hill-sized pile of used clothes—from a guy he knows in the wholesale business, some kind of rag dealer. The clothes seem okay, useable, but looks can be deceiving.

I make a mental list of the pile's contents. A black bustier in a child's size 2M; a wispy blouse that appears at first glance to be leopard print but is actually owls; Ziggy Stardust shoes; acid green, poly-plaid golf pants (real beauts, Jimmy says, but too small for him), with a matching green Nebraska Tech College t-shirt; a purse with tags still attached; a red, faux-leather, trench coat, à la Audrey Hepburn; tennis shirts from the Bruce Jenner collection; assorted western style shirts, the snappy kind.

Jimmy says that he isn't selling his business after all, the pile of new clothes apparently the culprit for his optimism. Not to be a naysayer, but I'm not sure there is a thousand dollars' worth of merchandise in his pile, even with the fetching owl-print blouse. Obviously it makes him happy to think otherwise, and things are looking up from his previous month's "donation" to the local Lummi tribe— AKA the casino's craps table—so who am I to rain on his parade? While I'm relieved he isn't bailing out this week, next week could be different. Eventually, the property management is going to want their back rent, money that Jimmy professes not to have.

Jimmy relays how Paris Texas, the store next door, had been sniffing around his property the month before, and how he feels contemptuous of their hipster posturing, their empty brand of style. He thinks they pander to a faux counter culture, a type of trust fund street waif, which offends his sensibilities because Jimmy considers himself to be the genuine article. A large part of his clientele aren't posing as poverty stricken, homeless addicts and alcoholics, they are poverty stricken, homeless addicts and alcoholics. Many are Mission residents, or railroad car buddies, apparently. I want to say mostly men who are down on their luck, who possess hearts of gold, but that'd be a cliché. A pair of Alaskan Natives appear on the sidewalk in front of the store and Jimmy rushes out to greet them, slapping one guy on the back and mumbling something about stolen lands and Custer. The pair and others drop by the store frequently throughout the day because Jimmy gives them cigarettes, and all that's required in return is that they stand still long enough for Jimmy to tell them a funny story.

For me, Jimmy represents the quintessential everyman's man, champion of the underdog. I admire his contempt for capitalism and corporate sellouts. Part of what drives his decision not to sell the store, he says, is that his retail neighbor wants the space so they can expand, and he takes delight in denying them what they want. As if he's staying afloat just out of spite. (As he once said, "If someone told me I couldn't be a Roman Catholic priest, I would be!") At one point, he posted a sign in the window—written on the back of a poster for *Beat Angel*, an independent film he starred in—voicing his disdain, and informing his patrons that the rumors weren't true: *Not Selling Out to Paris Texas!*

Scanning the expanse of the store I ask him where his Goth girl clerks are, and he says they're probably tired of being paid only in clothes, adding that his employees are the only reason he's able to stay afloat, because unlike him, they aren't constantly wheeling and dealing and slashing prices on a whim. He regularly greets his customers with a rousing "everything's half off! More if it looks good on you!" He's excellent with his regular customers: they'll wander in and he directs them to their preferences and sizes—like a good bartender who always remembers the customers' usual. A man and woman come in and ask whether Jimmy has any leather chaps. The man is unusually tall, and the woman is unusually short. Some days the Blue Moon looks like the set of a Fellini picture. Jimmy pushes a cart of clothes free for the taking out to the sidewalk. He says proudly that Bellingham has the best-dressed homeless in the country, largely due to him.

*

Friday, May 8, 2004. 9:30 AM. Bellingham, WA.

I've arranged to meet Jimmy for a hunting and gathering errand to Skagit Valley thrift shops. The ironic t-shirt and trucker caps department is running critically low, and he's out of vintage slips. We made plans to restock. He doesn't have a car or a license, so I offered to help him out. Jimmy complains, "No one dresses up anymore." He's referring to the eighties, the thrift store glory days of Bananarama and Cyndi Lauper, that magical decade when New Wave celebrants and hold-overs from the UK punk scene dressed up like serial killers or Ringling Bros. Circus clowns, the times before irony ruled supreme.

Jimmy phoned at 8:00 to set our meeting back to 9:30, something about a gutter man. Good title for a book: *Waiting for the Gutter Man.* I don't ask. When I get to the store to pick him up, Jimmy's sitting on the curb studying his shoes and gripping a brown, paper sack, filled with not alcohol but a collection of his personal effects: money, checks, ID, comb, etc. He blows into my car like a cyclone hitting a cattle barn.

As the car sits idling in the drive-in bank, I worry that we look like rookies in a drug cartel. A couple of ill-prepared, clumsy mules. The passenger floor is littered with checks and twenty-dollar bills, loose cigarettes, and change. Jimmy loses the pen, he can't manage to sign his name legibly, can't find his ID—it's a hot mess. Then he insists we visit McDonalds for breakfast, which delights him because he apparently doesn't have access to fast food restaurants living downtown—he also looks forward to asking the drive-thru window guy if fellatio comes with the Happy Meal, or rather the Happy Ending Meal, as he's decided to call it.

We stop off at the grocery store where Jimmy buys a can of Crisco. I can't imagine why anyone would want to buy a giant can of Crisco before 10 A.M., but again, it's better not to ask. In addition to the Crisco, he feeds dollar bills into the scratch-ticket machines, and buys a seven-dollar gadgety lighter shaped like a rocket that shoots out sparks.

Our first stop is a retirement home thrift store somewhere near Stanwood. It's dollar bag day and Jimmy, self-assured and in his element, gives off a heady note of swagger. What's better than Norwegian geriatrics and the musty clothes of the recently deceased? Each item has a story to tell and we're intent upon keeping a running commentary. 1) The needlepoint kit resembling a flattened possum:

"Nothing says Home Sweet Home better than a framed cross stitch of road kill." 2) The ribbon and plastic flora bound books: "An anti-literature craft project for wayward readers." 3) The Costco-sized bottle of lotion which was too expensive and put back on the shelf: "There goes your social life, Jimmy."

After stocking up with several grocery sacks of items, Jimmy nearly enters into a physical altercation with some blue haired dame in a sunflower headband. From what I manage to piece together, the proprietors are pissed about his being a messy, inconsiderate slob. Apparently, on a previous visit, Jimmy carelessly abandoned clothing items all over the aisles, on the floor, left them stranded on chairs, and forgot his baskets of items beneath the racks. The blue haired woman chews him out and good; Jimmy's been shop-shamed. Not that it's the first time, I'm sure.

"Yeah, but I bought like nine bags of clothes." Jimmy says to the lady. Nine dollars; I'm sure they really appreciated his business.

"Well, it probably wasn't you, but the man you were with, then?" Blue hair lady offers diplomatically. I guess she's referring to Bill, Jimmy's so-called biographer, a guy who keeps tabs on Jimmy's activities and helps promote his writing and acting career.

Next stop: Camano Island for another dollar bag sale. That Jimmy—he really has a finger on the pulse of second hand goods! We're greeted in the parking lot by a jaundiced man with a lopsided scar on his face and a silver hook for a hand. He appears to be the shop's fix-it man. Jimmy really works up a froth inside the store, telling the proprietors that he's picking up for clothing charities, like Evergreen Youth Home—at one point I overhear him telling one of the clerks that he's a priest and is picking up clothes for orphans at Paulie Shore's House of Casserole, which the clerk assumes is some kind of restaurant. We cram more grocery bags into the trunk of my car. I suggest gingerly that he might consider holding off on the shorts and tank tops and concentrate on adding to his winter/fall departments; a problem since Jimmy seems mostly interested in buying trucker caps, t-shirts, and polyester men's suits. Stuff *he* wears.

Jimmy naps most of the way home. When he does manage to stay awake he finishes his McDonald's sandwiches, tries reading part of a brochure on northwest salmon out loud in a variety of celebrity impersonations, smokes a couple of cigarettes, and in his customary Jimmy style holds forth on a critique of western civilization and his growing up in Queens as an Irish Catholic altar boy. He regales me with names and descriptions of all his homeless buddies, his married girlfriends, his epic drinking binges once upon a time on the Blackfeet Rez, and tells me about his partner in poetic crime sprees, the Lakota poet Luke Warm Water. Then he falls back asleep and a few minutes later awakens with a startled "HEY, BABY."

When we pull into Bellingham I take an inventory of the inside of my car, which now resembles the nest of a very large and messy bird—strewn newspapers, pamphlets, receipts, spilled bag of chips, crumbs in every crevice, cigarette ashes, scratch tickets, leftover McDonald's bags, used Kleenex, and the Safeway card Jimmy claims is his only form of ID.

*

I first met Jimmy at an independent film festival in Burbank. Jimmy played a spoken word poet in the aforementioned *Beat Angel*, an independent film about Jack Kerouac coming back from the dead. In it, Kerouac's spirit lands in the body of a hobo bumming for spare change during a poetry open mic held in celebration of Kerouac's birthday. The filmmaker was from Bellingham, as were many of the actors and crew. Jimmy's role was brief, just a flash compared to the rest of the film, but I must have watched and re-watched his scene dozens of times. He was so charismatic. He wore a *Mad Men*-style light-colored suit and a matching fedora. He was smoking a cigarette as he recited one of his original poems, I don't remember which one, it could have been from one of his chapbooks—"It Takes a Whole Mall to Raise a Child," or "Women are from Venus, Men are from Bars." On the back covers of his chapbooks more established poets wrote glowing reviews of Jimmy's work, saying he wrote in the tradition of Jack Kerouac, or Charles Bukowski. One of his bios described him as having worked as a bouncer on the Blackfeet Indian Rez, as a welfare cheat, and as a plasma donor.

In Burbank during the film festival and within just a couple of hours of meeting him, he barged into my hotel room with all the grace of a jacked-up Billy goat, jumped excitedly from topic to topic, picked up and handled most of my books and personal items, asked dozens of questions, paced from room to room, even checked out my closet, "NICE ROBE, I COULD SELL THESE," before scrambling out the door as if he was making a critical run for a toilet. That was his style. Hyper-mania. And it often left me feeling ramped up and exhilarated, like some kind of electrical storm just touched down, but the kind that made you feel lucky it picked you to visit.

After *Beat Angel* premiered at one of the cinemas in Burbank, a group of us drove around, stopping off at different bars and small clubs. Outside one of the clubs, Jimmy introduced himself to a potpourri of hipsters smoking outside. He made the rounds, shaking everyone's hand saying, "I'm Jimmy Henry, I'm a janitor at Hollywood High, I live in my parent's basement and I collect gay bondage porn." And then later at another restaurant he offered to buy my friend and me a drink. But he didn't have any money, so he told us he'd be right back and left to busk for spare change.

*

Sunday, April 11, 2004. 10:00 AM. Bellingham, WA.

I've been home a week after getting back from Burbank, and I happen to be hanging out at Stuart's, the coffee shop just around the corner from Jimmy's store. I'm sitting in the upstairs balcony at Stuart's when I notice movement coming from the area across the length of tables at the wall opposite me. I look up from my book and watch in astonishment as a rather large section of the wall is removed from the inside, then crashes to the floor. Next, a tall man in polyester plaid pants scuttles rodent-like through the hole and steps casually into the coffee shop, brushing himself off in a resolute kind of way before he turns back to the wall section, hoists it up, and fits it back into the wall like a piece of a life-sized jigsaw puzzle.

It's Jimmy. He has his own secret entrance from his apartment above the Blue Moon onto the balcony of Stuarts. When he notices me sitting at the table across from the crawl space, my jaw hanging open, he holds his finger to his lips, then nods hello, says he'll be back, before disappearing down the stairs to grab his morning coffee and pace up and down the street out front, smoking cigarettes and chatting people up.

This is how we become friends—or how I become Jimmy's personal ATM and chauffeur. We exchange phone numbers and make plans to listen to music at the Grand Avenue that night. He doesn't show up.

*

It's no great associative leap to say that Jimmy was Neal Cassady incarnate. For one thing, he never stopped talking. And it seemed like most everything he said was either pee-your-pants riotous or some deep, philosophical truth, like a soothsayer, a soothsayer with a laugh track. A shaman with mic. When I told Jimmy that his vagabond life of riding the rails, eating in missions, and sleeping on the streets should be made into a sitcom, he immediately said, "Yeah, a sitcom called 'Honey, I'm Homeless!'"

My money and resources seemed to swiftly disappear around Jimmy. But I continued hanging around him for the hilarious things he would say. Once, when he stood me up for about the hundredth time, his excuse was that some old railroad car buddies were in town and they insisted he drink with them all night. Railroad car buddies. As if he just stepped out of a page from The Grapes of Wrath, on his way to the land of milk and honey. He sometimes referred to his sexual encounters as "untying the Boy Scouts," a euphemism meant to corrupt what's wholesome or innocent, as in, "I took this high school girl who works in the store to a fancy party, a fundraiser, and after we drank wine and sampled the cheese platter, we went back to my loft and untied the Boy Scouts." I asked, "Oh, did she wear a backpack? Did she color at the table?" Jimmy once said that when he visited schools to present his poetry, his then-wife, Marilyn, insisted on accompanying him. "Like she was afraid I'd run off with a cheerleader or something." He joked about a junior-squad cheerleader being too old for him.

Jimmy was decidedly feral. He was the sort of person who would phone you up at three o'clock in the morning on what seemed to be a drug-induced manic jag, in order to read you a poem newly scrawled out in what I imagined might be a purple crayon. Or for a more serious occasion, to bail him out of jail. It also goes without saying that despite all this, I liked him immediately, until the day I decided I didn't like him anymore. Or couldn't afford to. Because aside from the charming aspects of his personality, his humor, his energy, Jimmy could also, quite often, be insufferable.

The last time I saw Jimmy was sometime just before he lost his business and left town with plans to bicycle across America. He invited me to drop by his loft to say goodbye. While I sometimes thought he might have a drug habit I never knew for certain, but the unmistakable glass pipe and butane torch sitting atop the coffee table like a gritty still life subject confirmed my suspicions. I didn't hear from him ever again, but a few years ago I found an article on the internet from some website out of Duluth that explained how Jimmy had spent the last few years of his life living there as the unofficial barstool poet laureate.

*

Monday, April 3, 2004. 9:00 PM. Burbank, CA.

Jimmy gets back to our table, with money to buy us drinks and appetizers. He tells us he recited poetry on the street to raise the cash. While we sit and enjoy our panhandled drinks, our begged-for appetizer, he pens "tattoos" on himself with a Sharpie. On the knuckles of one hand he writes "LOVE," and on the knuckles of his other hand, "HATE." On his left arm he writes "Mama Tried."

—<o>—

Senior Time

Kelly Froh

I'm a failure.

In many ways.

I've been laid off from several jobs. The last time I asked for it. I literally said, "Let it be me."

I left the office and vowed never to dress "business casual" again. I dumped four pairs of worn thin black pants into the nearest donation bin. I also stopped shaving my armpits, why not?

That job was killing my body. My knees pulsed with unearned pain. My lower back was in a constant throbbing knot. I said to people as a joke, "I'm the same shape as my office chair!"

I still sit a lot, but in a lot of different seats.

I started my own small business. I sit with seniors in their homes and we talk about what's on their minds, and the latest shooting, and if Donald Trump could really win.

I go buy their groceries. Sometimes we take a walk. I balance their check-book, do some dishes.

"See you next week!"

I sit on the bus. On the 8, 5, the D, and the E; the 10, 21, and the 44 to the 43.

On Fridays, I host "Coffee Corner" at a nursing home and try to make it fun despite having to serve lukewarm decaf. I have a list of topics and I fire them off one by one until someone is engaged enough to speak—

"Yeah, I was at the Seattle World's Fair, it wasn't that great."

"The worst thing to have happened to Seattle is when it started calling itself a city instead of a town."

On Mondays, I run an art class for seniors. I suggest to one lady to maybe paint some clouds in the sky and she says, "Where?" and I say, "Up there, at the top" and she does it, but then says, "Now what?"

One of the best students in the class is blind. She asks me where her colors are and I describe the palette: red at noon, blue at 3, yellow at 6. She paints wildly for 10 minutes then shouts, "DONE! (pause) Do you see the red butterflies, flying sideways, and the kitchen with the blue drawers?" "I see them," I say, and I do, mostly.

Sometimes I teach kids how to make comics, or, I try to.

"What are we doing this for?"

"So you can express yourself creatively and feel the satisfaction of making your own little book."

Later, I pick up the comic left behind on the table and it's mostly blank except for the center pages that read,

"Hate You."

When I'm not doing these odd jobs, I sit at home at my laptop with my electric heater burning quietly beside me. I think about drawing, but instead I reply, forward, like, comment, schedule, create Google docs, and try to mark off items on my "to do" list. I spend more time organizing art events than making art myself.

That wasn't really the plan when I volunteered to help organize a small, one day comics fest 5 years ago.

Now my partner and I plan festivals two years in advance because of grant deadlines and we text ideas back and forth no matter the time of day. My boyfriend told me to stop telling people that I didn't have a real job, or that I was still officially unemployed. But to me, unless it was 40-hours a week routine drudgery, it didn't feel like something I could claim. I am finally working in the arts, in a way I never expected.

"Dear Applicant, this is your third and final warning, if you do not pay by the end of the day, we will have to give your table away."

"Dear Donor, as you likely well know, being a nonprofit does not mean that we don't desperately need your money…"

All these actions used to be sneaked in at the office, when an eight-hour day was endless—when the time it took to get to noon was a whole day in itself, and after 3 pm felt like several. I'd look down at my outfit and think, "OMG I'm wearing the same clothes I wore on Monday. Oh wait, this is Monday… still."

I'm making less money now at 41 than I did at 21, but I feel I am doing my greatest work. I am piecing together a living with four jobs and time is speeding away like it doesn't want to be near me. I feel like I am always working, even when I'm obviously just watching TV.

"I feel like I am going die, Kelly."

"Well, you are. But probably not for a few more years."

We toast with little cups of green tea, "To NOT having cancer!" and then joke about the good looking Safeway pharmacist and how he could give us a flu shot anytime!

Perhaps I'm now on senior time, since I'm so often in their world. Is there something coming up behind me? What is that in the distance? It's two parts anxiety and one part 'eh, ...who cares'.

"What are we doing now?"

"I'm wheeling you down the hall."

"To where?"

"Your room."

"Then what?"

"Maybe you'll watch TV, or eat a Reese's Peanut Butter Cup."

"Then what?"

"Well, maybe you'll get tired and take a little afternoon nap."

"Then what?"

"Then you'll eat dinner, maybe talk with your neighbors for awhile."

"Then what?"

"Then, it's bedtime and you'll fall asleep and have a long, vivid dream of a full life; of childhood, and playing, and growing up, learning, coming into yourself, successes and failures, finding something you are good at that you can call your job, challenging times, good and bad but always meaningful relationships, places visited, meals eaten, homes cared for, pets, books, time alone—a life filled with lots of love and happiness."

"Then what?"

"Then, you die."

—<o>—

"Orchard District, Wenatchee River, near Cashmere, Washington."
Circa 1920s. U.S. National Archives.

An Interview with Amanda Coplin

Interviewed by Amy Wilson · October 2016

Amanda Coplin was born in Wenatchee, Washington and raised amid her grandfather's orchards. Her debut novel *The Orchardist*, set in the Wenatchee Valley around the turn of the twentieth century, was a *New York Times* bestseller and was named a best book of the year by National Public Radio, *Publishers Weekly* and *The Washington Post*. Coplin is a recipient of the Whiting Award for emerging writers and was selected by Louise Erdrich as a National Book Foundation 5 Under 35 honoree. *The Orchardist* has attracted particular acclaim from Northwest audiences and critics, winning the 2013 Washington State Book Award and the 2014 Reader's Choice Award from the Oregon State Book Awards. Bonnie Jo Campbell wrote of the book, "To read this mysterious, compelling, elemental novel is to immerse yourself in the world of an old folk song." Coplin recently relocated from Portland, Oregon to Vermont.

—◇—

Interviewer

The Orchardist is a work of historical fiction about a region and a moment that are seldom depicted in contemporary literature. Reading it as a Pacific

Northwest native, I felt a sense of groundedness that I don't usually feel with other works about American history. The Northwest is often portrayed as a destination or a landing, the end of a trail or a journey, but in *The Orchardist* the region is the starting point, the point of return, and the boundary of experience for the characters. How did you decide to write *The Orchardist* as historical fiction? And how do you see the novel's relationship to both Pacific Northwest history and to the larger fields of American history and historical fiction?

Coplin

I spent my early childhood in the Wenatchee Valley, often in the company of my grandparents who owned orchards there. In the summers they would pack us grandchildren in their camper and we would meander around the state, stopping at all the historical sites. Their interest in regional history, and the history of the Pacific Northwest at large, rubbed off on me, without question. I often wondered what the landscape was like before the advent of the orchards. I didn't realize until I began writing *The Orchardist* the extent to which that moment in history—the landscape on the cusp of major agriculturalization, at the turn of the last century—fired my imagination.

I didn't set out to write a work of historical fiction, per se. I value historical fact—of course—but I don't consider it to be the cornerstone of my work as a novelist, as writers in that genre do. It's more important to me, for example, to successfully depict the atmosphere of the place I'm writing about, and how the characters' interior lives relate to others' and events. Not that it's impossible to achieve both this and historical accuracy—they are not mutually exclusive—but I just don't value historical fact in the way that other die-hard historical fiction writers do, and that's an important distinction to make, I think.

As for how the novel relates to actual history—I was certainly playing with tropes of the American West, but beyond that, it's not for me to say. Let critics decide.

I'm curious to know which tropes of the American West you were playing with, consciously.

Coplin

Well I realized early on that Talmadge could be considered a kind of cowboy—a strong, silent type. But of course we come to understand that these perceived qualities come not from allegiance to some masculine code but rather from a lifetime of managing complicated grief. One reader said that Talmadge is the most stereotypically maternal character in the book— I thought that was interesting. It's true, though: he cooks for the girls, he constantly focuses on building them nests—literally. His constant fretful concern. The way he gently nags Della to be a better person, to come back home, to let herself be embraced by the structure of the family. Hardly the cavalier, macho type. And the fact that he sets out to "save" these girls, Jane and Della—that is a trope in itself, the man swooping in to save a couple of young females. I mean, the most optimistic reading of this is that he somewhat succeeds in helping Della. And he "saves" Angelene in that he offers her love and relative stability, at least for a short time. But he plunges her into grief, too, at different times. In my opinion these women save themselves—or, rather, they take their fate into their own hands. It doesn't even occur to them to give Talmadge that power, though they may—I'm thinking of Angelene here—love him.

Also, with the focus on horses—I wanted to go beyond treating them as props, I wanted to draw them deep into the narrative, so that they became part of the foundational humus of the novel. I wanted the reader to feel the ancientness of horses, of what they have meant to humankind over the ages—both practically and imagistically. Also, they are majorly important to Pacific Northwest native culture, and I wanted to emphasize that here, I wanted the horses to work as a kind of point of synthesis between the native culture and different themes of the book.

"Farm buildings and orchards at Eckert's ranch, Washington."
1904. University of Washington Libraries.

I could go on—I'm especially interested in what you said about the West being regarded in the larger cultural imagination as a destination, the end of a trail. I think there is great romance and beauty to this idea, but it is inadequate—inauthentic, really—to the place itself. What the place wants to say is something else, something greater. I don't know what it is, but writing is one way to get at it. I expect, and hope, that the literature of the place in the years to come will reflect this authentic voice in various ways.

Interviewer

How would you describe your relationship to the Pacific Northwest, as an individual and as a writer? You've lived both inside the region and outside— how do you find your physical location affecting your thoughts and feelings about the Northwest?

Coplin

The Pacific Northwest created my imagination. From the beginning, even before I knew what I was doing, I was constantly, obsessively attempting to translate the landscape into words, trying to frame and shape my experience.

Whenever I'm away from the Northwest, I am homesick for it, and this can sometimes help my writing. There is that story about Hemingway, that he wrote about Michigan best when he was in Florida, or Idaho. I can't remember the quote exactly—but it implies that we must have distance— physical distance—from the beloved place in order to see it clearly. On the other hand, there are advantages of living in the landscape of which you write: to be a witness to it in the present moment, to love it and honor it with your physical self, and also to be able, by your presence, to contribute in other ways to the community. I've been thinking a lot lately about my responsibility as a writer who cares so much about landscape—as a writer who places landscape as the central concern, artistically, in my work. Do

I have a responsibility to live in the Northwest? I don't know. I wrote *The Orchardist* mostly while living in Minnesota and Cape Cod. I think the immersion in other landscapes forced me to envision my own—that of the orchards of Central Washington primarily—and of course this isn't a bad thing. Now I live in Burlington, Vermont—I moved here because my partner got a job here. Vermont is beautiful. But I'm uneasy, being so far from the Northwest.

Interviewer

You've said, "there's something powerful that happens when you read about the specific place where you're from, and about the people who live there." What in particular was important to you to capture in writing about the Pacific Northwest? In writing *The Orchardist*, did you see the work as specifically regional?

Coplin

I think first and foremost I was intent on capturing a particular atmosphere—it is difficult to describe, and that's why I wanted to do it, to set up that project for myself. There is an atmosphere there—I'm talking about the orchards, being in the orchard aisles themselves, but also how the hills look against the sky; and the silence, and the odors of different seasons. I wanted to capture all that. I wanted to write about the ocean, too, the Pacific Northwest coast—that was a mythic place out of my childhood. I yearned to write about that as well, even if for a short span in the book.

In terms of seeing *The Orchardist* as specifically regional—sure. Does this mean that people living outside the region will not understand what I'm writing about? Of course not. What people respond to is the emotion encapsulated on the page. So often "regional" is a dirty word, but I've never understood that. I hope works are regional: I want to read an insider's view of what's going on. Don't you? I remember reading Alistair MacLeod's story collection Island for the first time, and being awestruck not only by his prose, but also by the evocation of place. He wrote about Nova Scotia, his home. His intimate knowledge of the region was his great strength.

Interviewer

I do want to read an insider's view! I think "regional" is sometimes falsely understood to be at odds with "universal." It's also hard to ignore the political aspect of the word, in that only certain regions are perceived as having "regional" qualities. It's interesting that you bring up the interlude in the novel on the Pacific Northwest coast, which was also a mythic place in my childhood. I really felt a sense of difference in the text in that section—the sense of expansiveness and softness, or even humility, that the Northwest coast inspires. Even within the "regional," there are so many textures to any place.

Coplin

I couldn't agree more. And I think what you point out here about textures is right. What's so interesting and rewarding about studying one particular place—one could also say the same about a person—is that you see beyond surfaces, which might be stereotypes or assumptions, and perceive what's beneath: differences, even contradictions, paradoxes. This makes people wildly uncomfortable, of course. That is why it is so often difficult to focus beyond stereotypes: because the true thing is variable, and unable because of its complexity to "fit" into boxes we have prepared for it. That's why the sustained focus of art-making is so vital, both to the health of our imaginations, but also society at large. A thing needs to be constantly re-imagined to be understood properly.

Interviewer

You've spoken in interviews about your sensitivity to "the desire to get something down just right, to generate emotion by arranging particular words in a particular order." This clarity of expression is evident both in the prose of *The Orchardist* and in the themes of intuition and silence that define parts of the book. What does it mean to write about silence? Do you ever experience any tension related to the ability or inability to express your thoughts in writing and if so how do you manage it?

Coplin

The simplest answer is that I wrote about silence because most of the characters are so extremely reticent. Mostly they are this way by temperament, but also they do not wish to disturb the great thing at the core of their lives that gives them trouble. To me the main challenge of writing about silent characters, and passive characters, is figuring out how to generate tension and drama. There is much passive action in the novel—people are physically laboring, they're traveling between destinations, they're in an orchard or garden working, thinking, remembering, speculating. This is what drives the movement of the novel. The pace is slow, but that's the point. When most of the action is passive, the violence is especially startling. And that's what I wanted to underscore too, the fact that the characters are most of the time surrounded by outer calm, performing their duties, and then suddenly they are engaged in, or forced to witness, terrible violence. I wanted to write about these extreme states of being—passivity and quietness, and violence.

In terms of feeling tension about getting thoughts down on the page—for me it helps, especially in the beginning, the early drafts, to just let myself go, give myself lots of space—and time—in which to explore on the page what I'm thinking. This is how the book becomes itself—from this letting out (drafting/writing) and pulling back in (reading over what I have written with a critical eye, cutting, revising, etc.). I engage in this back and forth until a shape emerges, eventually. This takes a long time, at least for me. I always err on the side of casting my net farther and wider than is probably necessary, a process that takes longer but ultimately yields more interesting material.

"Fishermen horse seining for salmon on the Columbia River."
Date unknown. University of Washington Libraries.

One aspect of *The Orchardist* that I found remarkable, and that many reviewers commented on as well, is the psychological depth of the characters. From a writerly standpoint, what's your approach to your characters' internal lives? For you is this the work of the imagination, is it observation, is it analysis, or is it something else entirely? I'd also love to know your thoughts on the role of the internal in writing more generally.

Coplin

The characters are formed from people observed throughout my life, but the process of creating them and accessing their internal lives is rooted entirely in the work of the imagination, especially in the beginning. Later, when I'm revising, or working with a critical reader or editor in trying to improve the work, there might be some conscious character analysis going on. Sometimes, of course, as a writer you get stuck—you get confused about a character, or you can't see an action clearly or you can't follow a certain emotion as it develops, or tries to reveal its source. Sometimes, for whatever reason, you cannot see. That's where a careful reader or editor will come in and offer suggestions. In terms of the approach to my characters' inner lives, in the beginning—usually I begin with an image or action, something visual and exterior, and then I write into it, and see where it goes. If I try to write into a character and something feels off somehow, I just try over and over again, until something reveals itself. Or, if I'm really stuck, I'll step away from it—this is so difficult because I would rather just keep hammering away at it—or I'll talk to someone about the problem I'm having. These things work out eventually, but an ungodly amount of patience is required, often.

When I first started writing *The Orchardist*, there was no interiority at all—I was trying to emulate Cormac McCarthy, who is so adept at relating emotion through exteriors. I admired his style so much, and still do. But I chafed against that way of writing, ultimately, and had to forge another method. I found a point of view and a tone, a voice, that suited what I wanted to say. The approach I used mostly had to do with tracking how a character moves through the physical world, moves through physical space, landscape, and performs physical acts and engages in relationships—with the land, animals, and humans—and how all of these objects act as triggers and cues for an internal play of thought, memory, emotion. To be able to track all this gracefully and at depth, all while showing a character or characters engaged in beautiful action, and then to make a shape for the whole thing, a shape that understands the story it is trying to tell—well that is the whole aim of novel-writing, of fiction, I think.

Interviewer

So much of what we think about when we think about setting in writing is about describing the way things look or are experienced externally—the way they smell, sound, feel, etc. Setting can be kind of passive in that way, as something that is objectified by being experienced. But by adding in the internal of "thought, memory, emotion", it's possible to achieve a new depth of setting by forging a connection to place that approaches the way it's actually experienced subjectively by an individual.

Coplin

That's an interesting way to think about setting—as symbiotic between place and individual. We often think of the physical landscape as drawing out a character's interiority, but what about vice versa? Would this be attributing a mind or consciousness to the landscape?

Do you know the work of the philosopher Maurice Merleau-Ponty? I think he has written about human creativity and the landscape along these lines. One of my favorite professors at the University of Oregon while I was an undergraduate there, Molly Louise Westling, wrote a book about Merleau-Ponty, *The Logos of the Living World*, where I remember reading about some of these ideas.

Interviewer

Another one of the most compelling aspects of the book for me person-
ally is the strength and tenderness of the relationships between Angelene,
Talmadge, Caroline Middey, Clee, Jane, and Della. These are highly un-
conventional relationships as they are neither sexual nor (for the most part)
biological. I'm curious as to whether this was something you approached
deliberately in structuring the book, or whether it was an outgrowth of plot
elements or something else. To put it in a more general way, in what sense
is *The Orchardist* about human relations to you and how do you see these
characters' relationships in context of the larger project of the book?

Coplin

One of the major themes of the novel is family—not so much in the biological sense, but in the sense of those with whom you fall in with, to whom
you are drawn, for better or for worse, with whom you settle even despite
constant psychological agitation. The novel is about, too, I hope, that truth
of how we deal emotionally with those family members who estrange themselves from us or even abuse us, or abandon us; they are not there, they cannot be physically accessed, but we must grapple with them in other ways.
How we have been treated by our original family affects those relationships
that we have later in life—of course. This is something, it does not have to
be stated, but in art we must be constantly reminded of this: if we do not
see clearly where we come from, the puzzle will present itself to us over and
over again, until we see, or until our blindness kills us. And often, especially
before we see clearly, we need people in ways that confuse and frustrate us.
It's exciting in fiction to untangle these relationships, to understand which
characters and situations echo others.

Interviewer

What about the relationship between the human characters and the natural world? Another *Moss* editor who read and enjoyed *The Orchardist* was

"Irrigating a 5-year-old winesap orchard near North Yakima, Washington." 1918. National Agricultural Library.

struck particularly by Della's fascination with the wild horses. Angelene is also occasionally represented as an embodiment or extension of the orchard itself.

Coplin

This focus on landscape reveals characters' interiority, certainly. I'm interested in how humans are connected to the physical world—beyond the obvious biological sense, but psychologically, spiritually, and in ways that are related to these things but cannot for whatever reason be defined. One of my favorite books is The Tree by John Fowles. It is a book-length essay, a meditation on the relationship between human interiority and wild landscapes. Fowles argues that it is essential to the health of our imaginations and spirits that such places exist in the world. And I believe it, not just theoretically, I feel it to be true from experience. When we encounter such places, we are uniquely moved. The experience is deeply, fundamentally, related to how we define ourselves as human.

Interviewer

Yes. I just read an interview with Barry Lopez by Nicholas O'Connell where he says, "The reason you go into unmanaged landscapes is in part to get out of a world in which all the references are to human scale or somehow devised from a sense of human values… it encourages you to think in a pattern that's nonhuman." He says it's a remedy for solipsism.

Coplin

Yes! And I'm so interested in these nonhuman patterns—and how they might inform literature, how we shape stories.

Speaking of Barry Lopez—there's an edition of *The Tree* with an introduction by him, and it's very good!

Final question! Who are your favorite writers of the Pacific Northwest, either historical or working today?

Coplin

The Haida myth-makers. Marilynne Robinson. Barry Lopez. Robert Bringhurst. Mildred Walker. Gary Snyder. Michael McGriff.

—◄o►—

Splitting the Sun

Gina Williams

In August of 1768, Captain James Cook set off from Europe on a journey commissioned by the Royal Navy to observe the transit of Venus across the face of the sun. "We took our leave of Europe for heaven alone knows how long, perhaps for Ever," he wrote. Captain Cook caught up with Venus in June of 1769 as her small, dark spot of a shadow split the sun. He recorded the two-day event in Tahiti after an eight-month voyage. Venus wouldn't be seen slipping across the sun's face again for more than a hundred years; the planet's transits are visible from Earth every 120 years, in June or December, in pairs eight years apart. Attempts to record the transit in 1761 had failed.

Almost exactly two hundred years later, on a hot, August night, my father would observe the transit of my mother's tears as she screamed from labor pains, and I was born, pulled from her womb with a medieval pair of metal forceps by a grimacing, thick-jawed Navy doctor. I was born six weeks early in the Whidbey Island Naval Base hospital, north of Seattle. My mother wasn't allowed to breastfeed, or even hold me, for weeks—a hospital policy as archaic as those forceps. For many days, I knew only the false warmth of a heated incubator, sugar water feedings, and the cold comfort of round-faced nurses who delivered sponge baths and diaper changes. "That rough moon landing made you tough, made you a fighter," my dad would later say, as he made shadow wolves howl and shadow rabbits hop on my bedroom wall at night. Did it? Am I?

Twenty-six years after that, on another warm, summer night, the goddess of love would split my heart as I rode on the back of a motorcycle with my boyfriend, the future father of my children. As we rumbled across a freeway bridge over the Columbia River from Oregon back to Washington State, the overhead lights on poles high above the roadway sent our shadows flying ahead of us. Our starkly outlined silhouettes whipped by in front of us again and again until we reached the other side, turned the corner, and descended into darkness. You could straddle a cycle right now, wait until sunset, and experience those leaping shadows on that same bridge. It might take your breath away. It might do nothing at all. But, for me, the surreal phenomena of watching ourselves repeatedly zoom away as our shadows were ripped by momentum and optics from our booted heels, flying away together into the night, made me cry with an inexplicable feeling of loss and longing. Maybe I somehow knew, even then, long before trying to make anything "work," that our fleeing shadows represented the impossible dreams that would leave us. Maybe I understood that shadows never lie, that shadow people never abandon one another, never pound their fists onto the kitchen counter in fits of marital rage, could never hurt a child.

The motorcycle was sold, eventually. It's been a long time since I choked back tears on the back of a Honda, lifted that plastic facemask a crack to get a gulp of fresh air, just enough to stop myself from reaching out as my outlined existence raced by, from making a futile attempt to grab hold of a ghost. Thankfully, my shadow did return, if reluctantly, and I keep it close by now, most of the time. It occasionally slips toward the moonlit windowsill and hovers there while I lie dreaming, but it doesn't get away for long. It makes just enough of a rustling noise, like fallen leaves blowing in the street to wake me. On those midnights, I sneak toward it stealthily and grab hold, keep it still while I stitch it, Peter Pan style, with a heavy steel needle and sturdy cotton thread, back onto my small, bare, twitching feet.

The word "photography" is derived from the Greek words for light and writing or drawing. To write with light is an attempt, I suppose, to net the soul of this life and the invisible fibers of our existence with shadows and illumination. Sometimes at night, I go for runs and walks alone in the city, looking for shadows to net with the camera obscura in my mind, indulging in the surreal, loosened world of lengthened light, double vision, and stretched reality. Chinese philosopher Mo Di knew of the camera obscura effect back in the fifth century B.C. He understood that light entering a pinhole could project an inverted image into a darkened room. He called it the "collecting place" and his "locked treasure room." I can escape there, in that collecting place, hiding inside of my own umbra, my total eclipse, even when it's nothing but the visual trick made by sodium lights dangling from poles in lieu of dark planets and blazing suns. Perhaps it is because my consciousness began in that shadowy realm that I enjoy retreating deeply inside of it now and then.

The mission of Cook's dangerous and risky voyage to view that speck of a planet shadow against the sun was to measure the size of the solar system, a cosmic question as important then as black holes and quantum physics are today. As early as 1716, astronomer Edmund Halley understood that Venus held a clue to the size of the solar system because the start and stop times of the transit, when recorded from different points on earth, could be used to measure by way of parallax or scale.

In spite of Cook's observations of Venus and the measurements made by others positioned across the globe in 1769, the exact size of the solar system still wasn't known; the fuzziness of Venus' atmosphere and the "black-drop effect," which caused the edge of the planet to appear to smear against the sun, made precise measurements difficult. Place your thumb and index finger near one eye and pinch them together. Just before they touch, you'll see the black-drop effect as a shadow bridge leaps between your fingers. It wasn't until Venus returned in 1874 and 1882 that photographers were able to accurately measure the transit, and the size of the solar system was finally ascertained.

In 2004 and 2012, I observed the transits of Venus on my television set and computer screen as images gathered by high-powered telescopes were broadcast via satellite. The goddess planet of love and beauty won't dot the sun again until 2125. I'll be a particle of dust by then, a whisper, a wink, my ashes strewn across the desert by howling winds. Thinking about the great explorers like Cook and our own astronauts, I wonder what I'd do, what I'd risk, to seek and find answers among the shadows, from the shadows. Maybe I'm tough, willing to fight and endure for some things. But I'm not brave, am I? If given the chance to see a new world, would I walk that plank? What voyage am I on right now that may reveal itself with answered questions long after I'm gone, like Halley, Cook, and Mo Di?

Yesterday, on an early morning, late summer stroll, my shadow stretched out in front of me on the sidewalk. I punched at it, jabbed at myself, did a few high kicks. My short legs doubled into long and stately shadow limbs in the rising sun. My edges appeared gilded. My shadow torso stretched into willowy elegance. My shadow hair flipped into an instant perfect style in the breeze. Then, I turned sideways in the soft morning light and disappeared into myself. For a moment, I hovered there and didn't really want to return.

—<o>—

Alabama

Kjerstin Johnson

Sean belted Neil Young's build-up over the empty floor of Hoagie Planet—
he was about to hit the best part of the best track on the album. But just
as he burst into the chorus, the music fell out, and his righteous blast of
"*Alabama!*" fell unaccompanied over the counter.

There was a clattering in the back. "Goddammit, Drew," he said,
right before the opening lines of *Straight Outta Compton* came over the
speakers.

Drew walked out of the kitchen. His shoulder-length surfer hair fell
into his face even though Sean had already told him to tie it back that
day. "We've been listening to your sad-sack shit for like, an hour. You said
I could play this when we were closing."

"We're slow, not closed." It was twenty til ten. And there were only
two songs left on *Harvest*! The Planet Hoagie door dinged open, giving
Sean the proof he needed. Drew slinked back to the kitchen and the loud,
caustic sound of an unplugged iPhone followed.

"This weather is nuts," said the man at the door, stomping snow-
covered shoes on the carpet without looking up. "Hey—Sean!"

"Lito, long time."

"Yeah man, I didn't know you still worked here."

"Oh, yeah. Well, managing now. I mean, yeah, I'm still working here, but also I became the manager. But, I mean, that was a while ago." Sean pushed up his glasses. "What can I get you?"

Lito squinted at the menu on the wall. "Footlong beefeater. No onions, thanks. It's so good to see you, man. I don't think we've seen each other since…"

"Probably since that show at Nate's."

"Oh yeah. That was a good time. I thought you guys would open for us some time. Didn't he work here too?"

"For a little bit. Before Brooklyn called."

"What's his new band called? It has a bunch of letters, I always forget. They're blowing up."

"Hatemail," said Sean. "Well, 'HTML.' They've got a Nikon commercial now." He trailed off. "Kinda stupid."

Lito shrugged. "Kinda funny. My new band is called 'the Rocky IV,' so I'm not sure I can talk."

"Oh. I was talking about the—" He heard the door ding open again. His face changed. "Hey, Naomi."

Instead of the size-L green Hoagie Planet tee Sean was used to seeing her in, the only one in stock when she started two weeks ago, she had on a regular shirt under her parka. She had two of those bird tattoos beneath her collarbones. "Hey," she said. "I just came to grab my schedule for next week." Sean had started making her a mix CD after she had asked about a Dinosaur Jr. song he had played last week. It wasn't anything serious— twelve 100% platonic tracks, no room to read anything else into it, not unless she wanted to. He hoped she wouldn't notice that they were working the same shifts.

Naomi headed to the kitchen and Sean turned back to Lito. "I like your name," he said. "You guys are good. Weren't you written up in The Weekly recently?"

"Yeah. It's just that Charles is leaving, and that's who they mostly talked to."

"Huh. That's cool, I mean—it's not cool. I'm sorry. For your band."

Lito shrugged. "He was okay. We're really happy for him." Lito was such a chill guy. "Hey! We're doing tryouts for a new front guy this week. You should come, Thursday's open. I know you've got the chops—I've seen you at Milo's."

Sean laughed and pushed up on his glasses.

"No I'm serious," Lito continued. "We need someone soon, too. We have a New Year's gig at the Central with Antler Spray."

Antler Spray sucked, if Sean was thinking of the right band. "Wow, thanks man. Let me think about it. I'm gonna see how that sandwich is going."

Sean stepped back in the kitchen where Drew and Naomi stood nestled against the dishwasher, Naomi smiling at Drew's stupid California face. The beef hoagie sat chastely on the mottled cutting board. With fanfare, Sean snapped a square of aluminum foil from the industrial size roll above the sandwich fixings. Drew casually looked back; Naomi jumped. "Got my schedule," she said, guiltily flashing a note-scribbled napkin at Sean as she slipped out, eyes down. Sean finished wrapping the sandwich.

"Naomi's giving me a ride," said Drew, grinning. "You know, the weather."

Back out front, Sean slid the sandwich to Lito. "Sorry about that."

"No, thank you! Glad I saw you. See you Thursday, I'll text you my address. Can't believe this snow."

"I can't believe it either," said Sean, watching Naomi thumb at her phone in an empty booth.

"Just bring your guitar, and maybe check out our Soundcloud," Lito called on the way out. Sean hoped Naomi heard. He played a *real* instrument, he didn't "make beats" or whatever the fuck Drew did. The door shut and N.W.A. began blaring from the speakers again.

"Okay kids," Sean announced loudly. "I'm gonna go count the till," and he took the registers upstairs to the office.

As he waited for Hoagie Planet headquarters to confirm the night's numbers, Sean opened a new browser to check his email. Two camisole-clad brunettes stared at him from a sidebar, offering to CHAT NOW FOR PORTLAND ORE HOOK-UPS. On a whim he clicked on the image, and was instantly assaulted by seven small windows billowing onto the screen.

"Hey man. Knock knock," said Drew at the door. "Hands where I can see them—ha, I'm just playin'." Sean quickly clicked around to close the pop-ups. "We're checking out, I just wanted to see... with the snow and shit... I don't have to come in tomorrow, right? Lots of places are closing up tomorrow."

"Like who?" said Sean.

"Lots of places! Have you seen the forecast? Go to Weather.com," Drew started toward the monitor and Sean quickly pressed a CLOSE icon, releasing a new flurry of hungry-eyed Portland singles over the screen.

"No. And yes, we're open. Nice try."

"Man I'm just saying, it's hard to get around without wheels."

"We have that Coke shipment coming tomorrow. My hands are tied."

"So wack," said Drew as he went out the door.

Sean finally closed all the errant windows. There was only one new message in his inbox, from OkCupid. SEANSTER11, SOMEONE CHOSE YOU! He hadn't logged in for months and was surprised he still remembered his password. The message was from a girl named Valerie. OkCupid said she was 26, she ate meat, and that she hated the question about what movie you could take on a desert island. Her music tastes weren't objectionable, either, but that just meant she didn't list HTML.

"Later big guy," Drew called from below. Naomi giggled at something he couldn't hear.

Sean clicked the reply button to Valerie and asked if she was free tomorrow night, maybe around eight.

The power went out at five the next day. Sean had just navigated to the Rocky IV's Soundcloud when he heard a tell-tale click and the living room flickered dark. His laptop screen glowed dully and he stared at their track list, completely unclickable.

"Power's out," said Jason, emerging from his bedroom. "I'm going to Teddy's."

Sean shut his laptop and walked toward the window. He pulled the blinds up, like the dark outside could light up the dark inside, just a little. Nothing moved outside except for the snow, which fell in sheets.

He sat back down and picked up his guitar from the futon. He had gotten as far as tuning it before getting online. He'd dicked around on Facebook—searching in vain for Valerie, spending too much time on Naomi's profile, and hate-browsing photos of Nate, whose flash-brightened face smiled back at him from parties in cramped apartments. When Nate left for New York in April, he and Sean had texted for a while—Sean asked Nate how he'd made the decision so easily, and Nate asked Sean why he couldn't just leave too. Sean had just renewed his lease and been offered the management gig at Hoagie Planet, and he couldn't really turn down the better hours and pay, especially since Careers—that, of all things, is what they had called their band—would no longer be booking shows. Nate hadn't even planned on moving—he just couldn't afford to fly back and had somehow made it work. He had asked Sean to visit, to at least bring the amp he had left in Portland. Sean had texted I would have to sell it to buy a ticket lol. Nate texted back: sell everything else and drive ya dummy.

That was all before the camera commercial. Jason was watching a baseball game when Sean got home from work. He had just opened a beer when he froze at the riff blasting from the next room. He walked slowly into the living room, where a bright, vivid commercial of sunflowers blooming and dancing cameras played chords he had once jotted down on a Hoagie Planet to-go menu, though they were now revved up in a catchy, two-tone synth number.

"What the fuck," he said, more shocked than mad. He watched a pile of puppies tangle on a beach.

"I know, it's like, why don't you fix your crappy 230 model before making an *extra* crappy 560," offered Jason.

"I wrote that," said Sean. "We wrote it. Here."

Jason grasped Sean's gravity for a short silent moment. "So you don't want to watch the game?"

Sean downed his beer. "I'm going to Milo's."

Now, in the dark, his fingers moved to the familiar frets. He plucked out the original melody, comically neutered on the unamplified instrument. It made him sad. He still liked the way the chords sounded. He played it through a few times, the way he had written it, pretending it had never been twisted three time zones away. He let the strings bite into his uncalloused fingers; the more it stung now the less it'd hurt later.

His phone buzzed. It was a photo text from Drew of the register's daily sales so far—$16.54. Drew had included a memo at the bottom for emphasis: 8===D~

Sean sneezed, realizing he was sitting alone in a dark room that was getting progressively colder. He got his coat and headed out.

The snow wasn't falling fast, just steadily, like it was pacing itself. The sky was an unfamiliar purple. With the wet soaking through his canvas shoes and his unlit block now foreboding in the pervasive darkness, he hustled the four blocks to Milo's, where the neon KARAOKE sign was caked in snow drift.

Sean's glasses fogged up the moment he stepped through the door. He wiped them off and ordered a double whiskey soda and a burger. At the bar, a glowing plastic Santa welcomed a busier-than-usual weeknight crowd—cold and confused refugees from the neighborhood. Sean wondered if his chances to sing tonight would be slimmer, then felt guilty about it. Another text from Drew: made 5 sammies all day. no coke.

He was on his second drink when a girl with dark, shoulder-length hair and cat-eye makeup walked over. Her face was flushed, like she had been outside for a while. "Sean?" she asked, head askew like he had done something and wasn't fessing up to it.

"Hi. Yeah, Valerie. I mean, I'm Sean, you're... Valerie. Hi." Sean ran his hand over his beard and stuck it out, then hesitated, then wiped his hand on his pants. Valerie just sat down.

"This weather is nuts. For Portland I mean."

"Yeah, I lost power at my place."

"Oh shit, really? We still have ours. I'm like ten blocks thataway," she said, nodding her head back toward the Santa. "Where do you live?"

"Pretty close, it's not a bad walk. It's like, 21st and Thorn. Between 21st and 22nd. Sorry, that was really specific, you didn't need that specific a location."

"That's funny, I work near there... The ugly brick building on 20th. My cousin's law firm." Without warning, Sean's body shivered and he sneezed.

"Bless you," said Valerie. "Did you only have a coat on? You realize they make products for problems like that. Hats. Gloves."

"Right."

"Sorry, I'm from Wisconsin. It's just second nature for me to have five layers on when it's cold out. I had to walk tonight—it's impossible to bike, and I don't have a car." Another biker. At least she wasn't vegan. Over at the bar, Sean saw the Nikon commercial come on the TV. He ran his thumb over the pads of his left-hand fingers under the table.

"So, you... do... legal stuff?"

"Well, it's sort of a temporary gig. But yeah, I do admin at this legal firm. Until I figure out grad school or something. Pretty sure I don't want to be a lawyer though. Not if it means going to work at 7:30 even when there's a psycho snowstorm."

Sean nodded sympathetically. "Sucks."

"What about you, do you have to work tomorrow?"

"Um... maybe? Guess we'll see what the weather's like?"

The KJ was setting up. Sean had finished his drink but didn't want to push another round on her, even as she stabbed at her ice cubes. She was looking at her watch. Fuck.

"Okay," said Valerie gravely. "There is only ten minutes of happy hour left. I need to get a drink *right now*. Do you want another?"

Sean adjusted his glasses. "Oh! Yeah, I mean, if you—I can—I mean, I have a tab—but, yes. Yeah I would."

"So… yes?"

"Yes," said Sean. "Thank you. I'll have what you're having."

The KJ placed a songbook on Sean's table. He realized he had torn his napkin into shreds and quickly wiped the tiny wet bits onto the floor.

Valerie returned with two amber glasses. "What's this?"

"Laaaaadies and gentleman welcome back to another karaoke night at Milo's. I'm your host Stevie B and we're going to get started with… Kaaaaatie! Katie come on up." Sean preferred it when Stevie B kicked things off—usually with Springsteen. It set a good tone for the night. It was important, like the first track in a mix CD.

Valerie turned back, "Did you know about this?"

"Well I—I mean, yeah—well it's *every* Wednesday so—but I didn't like, plot this. I mean… I come here a lot."

"I see."

"Do you… enjoy… karaoke?"

"Uh… well," Valerie cocked her head again. "I guess—well, I don't think I've done it. So I can't really say."

"Oh, it's the best. You'd be great at it." Katie finished her Nelly Furtado song to polite applause.

"Let's hear it for Kaaaaatie," said Stevie B. Steve was such a pro. "Now let's get Sean up here. Come on up *Sean*!"

Valerie made a "well look at you" face at him and he took a deep drink before heading up to the mic. The signature synth of "When Doves Cry" started up. He liked this song—it was a crowd pleaser. As he sang the first verse, he hit every innuendo without coming off too *American Idol*. He felt Valerie watching him, and even though he didn't need the screen, he found himself glancing at it to avoid her gaze. He nailed the closing Prince ad-libs, and growled them over the robot-chorus refrain.

"Thank you Seaaan! One of our Milo's regulars performing a little Prince for you fine folks. Next up we have…Cher…isa? Am I saying that right? Cherisa?"

"Bravo," said Valerie, when he returned to his seat. "I'm definitely not going to

go if you're the competition."

"It's not a competition!"

"Do you like, practice or something? You even made that little"—Valerie made a little Ow! sound, which, to be honest was a little more MJ than Prince—"sound pretty hot."

Sean ran his hand over his beard. "Thanks, it's just something I like doing."

"So you work at Hoagie Planet? My friend got sick there once." There was a pause. "It was the one downtown," Valerie added quickly. She flipped through the songbook. "I don't know any of these songs! I mean, I *know* Ace of Base but I don't want to sing them. Maybe if they had, like, Antler Spray, I'd sing that."

"Did you say Antler Spray?" said Sean.

"Yeah," she said, then gave him a look. "Don't give me any Pitchfork bullshit about them. I like them. A lot of people like them."

"No, I mean, well, I have only heard their older stuff—I mean, sorry I didn't mean it that way, I have seriously only heard one album by them and it happened to be their first one. What I mean is that this band—a band I'm in… we're actually playing with them—"

"*What.*" said Valerie. "Wait. The New Year's Eve show? If you are bullshitting me—if this some elaborate hipster joke I swear to god I am going to walk out of this bar right now."

"No, seriously. The Rocky IV. At the Central."

"Are you shitting me."

"…No?"

"I can*not* believe this. I'm texting my roommate." Valerie started typing on her phone. "She is literally going to slit her wrists about this. She is like, their biggest fan." Her phone chimed almost instantly. Valerie answered and whispered loudly "*It's her*" to Sean, pointing at her ear.

She walked to a quieter end of the bar and Sean ordered another round. He rubbed his left thumb around the pads of his fingers over and over. At the mic, a girl watched her Third Eye Blind lyrics reel by. "Whoa. I did *not* know these were the words to the song."

Valerie came back a few minutes later with her phone still cocked to her ear. "Hey, I'm trying to figure out work tomorrow. Where do you live again?" Sean told her, even though he didn't understand the question. Still… he texted Drew. k HQ says we're closed tomorrow.

Valerie returned and sat down. "Yikes," she said to Sean, nodding back at an older guy's off delivery of "I Can't Help Falling In Love With You."

"Yeah, I feel really bad when this happens. I don't even think this guy is a bad singer, he's just like, *one* note off-key, and he knows it, and he's just… clawing his way back."

Valerie kept her eyes on him as he spoke. She put her hand on her heart and in faux earnestness locked eyes with Sean. "Makes you wish there was something you could do."

"It's a heartbreaking, completely preventable condition," he replied in matched concern.

"So but seriously. Is that what you do—sing?"

"Well, I also write music. Figure out the song structure and chords before Nate adds lyrics and like… his pretty-boy production. Probably doing that in Williamsburg right now."

"Williamsburg? Like, New York? And he's coming to the show next week? My roommate tried to fly home and said the airports are a complete shitshow." Sean realized she hadn't been asking about Careers.

"I'm not worried about it," he said, and for the first time in a while, he really wasn't.

The drinks arrived. "Seannnnn, Sean if you could step up to the mic." Maybe he and Stevie B should be in a band together.

Valerie raised her eyebrows. "You're singing *again*?"

"I mean," Sean stared ahead at the microphone. "I can't go home. It's just…cold and roaches there." Valerie laughed. He hadn't said it as a joke but he was glad she liked it.

Pink letters reading *Sweet Talkin' Woman—in the style of Electric Light Orchestra* bled into a cyan screen. The strings started up and Stevie B put on a pair of sunglasses. "Don't know what I'm gonna dooooo," he crooned, stretching his arm out like total cheeseball, then drawing it back and clutching a fist—"I gotta get back to youuuu" he looked at Valerie even though he hadn't planned to. He had expected her to be browsing the songbook but she had been looking right at him with a bemused expression, and only glanced away when he caught her eye.

About halfway through the song Katie's table came to the dance floor. This was his favorite part of the song, when the music dropped out for two measures then kicked back in before things got too melodramatic. "Slow down—*slow down*—sweet talkin' Lola…" Sean received loud whistles when he was done.

"It's cold outside but let's keep things hot with a little R. Kelly from Robbbbbie," announced Stevie B. "Can we get Robbie up here."

After that the dancing never let up. Valerie even went up to sing some Gwen Stefani with an amorphous group of middle-aged women. When last call rolled around it seemed like the whole bar was on the dance floor, shouting along every word with Stevie B to "Hungry Heart." The room's warm red lights shone on everyone's face and the tinsel rippled on the wall. Outside, the snow plummeted, the flakes lit up by the orange glow of the streetlights, falling like sparks from a fire.

"The roof is on fire," he said.

"You're drunk," she said.

Then it was over. The house lights came on and Sean's damp t-shirt stuck coldly to his back. Over a clatter of glasses, "Comes a Time" came over the bar's speakers. Neil. "Do you know this song?" Sean slurred to Valerie. He was in love with Valerie. He was going to make a mix CD for her. It would have Neil, and Dinosaur Jr., and "Mama You've Been on My Mind"—the Jeff Buckley version. "I want to talk to you about this song. You can't hear it right now, you can't hear it right, but I need to tell you about it."

"I bet you do," said Valerie. They stepped outside. The snow glowed faintly pink from the bar's red Rainier sign. "Here, wear this," she gave him her wool hat. Then she grabbed his shoulders and positioned him East. "Lead on."

He turned to her, fat flakes falling on his face. "You're coming to my place?"

"I just think…" she blinked and her eye makeup left small black tracks on her cheek. "Sometimes it's nice to weather these things with someone else." The thought had never occurred to him. "Also I need to get to work in the morning."

When Sean woke up, he had a thick headache and a dry mouth. The snow had stopped, his phone was dead. The power was back. Valerie was gone.

He took a hot shower and grabbed the last High Life from the fridge. Cancelling work had been a great decision. Drew was a genius.

A sleeping bag folded in an oblique square sat on the futon. He moved it aside and it crumpled into a soft mess on the floor. He plugged his phone in and played through three Rocky IV songs before his phone buzzed to life. He made himself wait until he had finished the song before texting Valerie. **Had a great night. Am free tonight after band thing.**

When Sean had run through every Rocky IV song twice and had emptied his High Life, he shut his laptop. He looked at his phone, and at the sleeping bag, and out the window where everything was white and grey. He couldn't see anything when he looked back inside. He closed his eyes and let his fingers find their place for the Careers song again. Now amplified, the song seemed sadder, lonelier, with so much energy behind it but no backing band. Working slowly, he picked out a new chord, a bridge that chased the gloom with a knowing nod. He murmured a song with no words somewhere high above it.

At ten til two, his car didn't start. He counted out bus fare from the kitchen drawers. The snow that had sparkled last night now scrunched with contempt underfoot, and his feet were soggy when he reached the bus stop. A girl with huge headphones, maybe Naomi's age, was waiting too. She glanced reservedly at him when he approached.

Sean nodded at her and pulled out his phone and dialed the bus alert number. "Thank you for calling Tri-Met. WINTER. WEATHER. ALERT," annunciated the robot voice. "Arrival times may be indeterminate due to winter forecast. Number FIFTY. FIVE is FOUR minutes OR. TWENTY. ONE. minutes away."

Sean texted Lito. **Bus late. SO sorry. Be there as soon as possible.** He paused then hit backspace. **Be there asap.** He deleted everything. **Bus is late. Keep u posted.** He hit send.

"S'not coming," he half-said to the girl, throwing it out with a laugh for her to respond to or not, only then remembering her headphones.

She removed one earphone and he heard a thin, familiar strain of music. Was it—? Probably not. He couldn't. He wasn't that guy. She probably had a boyfriend. Why wouldn't she? What if she didn't? What was he doing? Valerie had come home with him last night.

"The bus," Sean threw his thumb back. "I mean," he held up his phone. "I called it, it's not coming. I mean, they said it was, but, like—the number, Tri-Met, said—I mean, usually when the weather is like this, it doesn't come.." He put his phone in his pocket. "Are you... is that *Harvest*?"

"What?"

"Are you listening to Neil Young?" But it was too late. He now heard plainly that what he had mistaken for the signature harmonica of "Heart of Gold" was actually a dark violin riff, a harsh and ugly melody warped through her headphones and this bullshit weather. "Nevermind,

I just thought I heard… Okay so this is funny because actually, the other night I was listening to, well, I mean I wouldn't *normally* care that you were listening to Neil Young—" He could hear more of the abrasive music now. "But you're not! So I don't—"

"It's Two Days Til Your Tombstone."

"Oh! Yeah," said Sean knowingly, like she had just asked if he was wearing clothes or if his body took food he ate and converted it into energy. He pushed up his glasses. "Wait, that's the name of the band?"

She had removed her headphones. "That's what you asked, right?"

"Yes, I did," said Sean.

"You said the bus isn't coming?"

"It's either really close or not coming." He shifted his guitar from one side to the other and ran his hand over his beard. "*So* not cool. I'm gonna be late for band practice." She gave him a tight smile and began scrolling through her iPod with her fingerless gloves. "I'm sort of the frontman, not sure what they can do without me right now."

"It's here," the girl said.

"Hm?" said Sean, leaning in.

"The bus."

He turned to see the 55 plowing over the white horizon in a wake of slushy refuse. "Right. Cool. Yeah." He pulled out his phone. nm. on my way.

It was 2:50 when he walked up to Lito's house. A birdbath filled with snow stood nearby, its bowl pockmarked with cigarette butts. Three empty PBR cans lay half-interred near the front steps.

He tried the door, but the wet brass knob twisted uselessly, making a whiny, tactile squeak. "Hey!" Sean looked up to see Lito's tapping at a window. "Sean! Try the back."

Inside it was warm and smelled like weed. Sean left his shoes in a pile of boots by the door and put his coat and guitar by a closet. He could still smell the wet metal of the doorknob on his hand. Five guys sat around a huge television playing *Call of Duty*. Sean recognized a few of them, he thought, although they looked like a lot of people. They were tall and trim, wore moustaches and North Face. He imagined they drove Jeeps and had girlfriends with names like Dakota and Taryn. An elegant, blown-glass bong sat on the table.

Lito glanced over at him. "Hey man. Sorry, a bunch of guys had work off today. We're getting a late start with practice."

"No worries," said Sean, crossing his arms and leaning on his right foot, then switching to his left. The men twitched and angled in front of the television. Sean wanted to comment on the game, but didn't know which trajectory to follow on the split screen.

His pocket buzzed. Valerie. Hey. Thanks for letting me crash! Busy tonight, have a good band thing :)

no worries, he typed. some other time :) Now he had time to finish her mix CD. He kept his phone out for a bit but she didn't text back.

"Ah fuckshit," said Lito. "I got shot. You want a turn, Sean?"

Sean said sure, though he now wished the 55 had never shown up, that he was still on the curb with Two Days Til Your Tombstone.

"Are we playing co-op?" Sean asked, mimicking what he had over-heard Jason say a few times.

"It's online."

"Cool," said Sean. "Cool cool."

Sean's camo-clad figure moved at an uncomfortably quick clip through a cement structure, feeling a sense of command and ineptitude at once. A figure appeared to his right. Sean shifted his sights, aimed, and fired something.

"Dude what the fuck?" said one of the guys.

"Oh shit, sorry," said Sean. "Did I get you killed?"

"No," said Chris, the casualty. "You got *both* of us killed because you threw a grenade." Sean stared at the screen, now turning crimson. He pressed on the buttons on his controller just to hear them click.

"I don't think the two of us can hold them off," said another guy. Lito exhaled a cloud of smoke "We should probably get started anyway. Ready to play yet?"

Sean checked his phone again as the Rocky IV extricated their lanky frames from the couch and descended to the basement. No new messages. Maybe he hadn't actually sent the last one? He clicked to his outbox. Okay, he had.

The basement was freezing. Chris settled behind the drum kit.

"What do you want to play, boss?" asked Lito.

"Uh… Well, I mean, I only know—I mean, what do *you* want to play?" They ran through some Rocky IV songs, Sean successfully coasting through the ones he didn't know the words to.

After a few songs Lito said, "Well you definitely don't sound like Charles, but that's not necessarily a bad thing." It felt good to be part of something again, to feel everything swell up around him, even if he tripped up a few times and his fingers felt a little wooden in the cold. Even if they were opening for Antler Spray.

"Okay, one thing we've been making people do," said Lito, "is show some stuff you've been working on that you think maybe we could all play."

"Sure, sure sure," said Sean. "Yeah, I uh, I do actually have something. It's uh," Sean quickly fingered the frets. "C major 7… B minor 7… then uh… D." He started at a slow tempo, finger-picking the song he hadn't shaken for two days. "Oh—hold on actually." Sean stopped and pulled out a glass slide. Its sound on the guitar seemed to cement what he had been going for, and after a few stanzas he looked up, almost surprised at himself.

Lito began a bass line beneath it and Chris eventually surrendered a simple beat. The confluence of sound spread a warmth he hadn't felt in a long time through his body. It carried him somewhere and a melody came to him that he hummed lightly, just off the mic. He closed his eyes and heard his song for the first time.

Lito seemed pleased. "Nice, man. How do you guys feel about it?" The keyboardist shrugged assent.

"Yeah, it's cool," said Chris. "Reminds of that one song—"

Sean interrupted. "Well actually *I*—I mean. Nate didn't even—this is what it was supposed to be." Sean stopped talking because he felt his voice tremor.

It was quiet for a second. "No I mean, it sounds like that one song. You know, *Duh nuh nuh nuh* lotta-love!" Chris sang flatly. "Same chords, right?"

Sean turned to face the drum kit. He thought he felt his phone buzz in his pocket but he left it.

"You guys know what I'm talking about, right? *Unhhuh unhhuh* lotta love… to get me through *dun-uh*. Who was that, Clapton?"

"Neil Young," said Sean. "It was Neil Young." He ran through the chords on his guitar slow and deliberately, the slide squeaky but clear. "You're right," he said, still staring at his fingers on the fret board, disappointed in their betrayal. He slipped the slide off.

Chris held out his drumsticks like he was shrugging. "I mean, maybe your song changes? I don't know."

Sean turned the volume down on his guitar but kept playing, humming something over the tinny sound of the strings. Then he stopped. "I don't know if it does."

Lito broke the silence. "I like that song, wanna make a go at it?"

Sean looked up, realizing where he was. "Yeah. You know, I actually have a shift at five… that I need to make. And it'll probably take forever getting over there… I better—I really appreciate you guys having me over. Good luck with auditions."

Outside Sean studied the bright, cold landscape in front of him. The small houses, the bicycles left locked to stop signs, the dog turds on the sidewalk—they all sat where they had been two days ago, only now they were enveloped indifferently by a soft three-inch layer of snow. He stood there until he heard a muffled drum beat come from the house he had just left, the real band practice starting, the sound swallowed up by the snow. Sean walked over to one of the snow-covered cars in the street and put his hand on the white-coated roof, pushing through the icy crust to the fluffy snow below. He left it there until it began to hurt.

—◦—

"Columbia River." 1913. University of Washington Libraries.

An Interview with Elissa Washuta

Interviewed by Alex Davis-Lawrence · October 2015 · Edmonds, WA

A finalist for the Washington State Book Award, Elissa Washuta is known for her deft, powerful, and deeply personal creative nonfiction. In her debut book *My Body is a Book of Rules*, Washuta uses a variety of forms and genres to grapple with issues of mental health, sexual assault, and personal identity; her followup, *Starvation Mode*, released as an eBook by Future Tense Books' new digital-only imprint Instant Future, focuses on her life's history of disordered eating. A recipient of grants and awards from Arist Trust, 4Culture, and Hugo House, her work has appeared in *Salon*, *Third Coast*, and *The Chronicle of Higher Education*, and she's worked as a contributing editor for both *The Rumpus* and *The James Franco Review*. A member of the Cowlitz Indian Tribe, she serves as an adviser for the Department of American Indian Studies at the University of Washington and on the creative nonfiction faculty for the Institute of American Indian Arts MFA program. Washuta currently lives in Edmonds, WA.

—◇—

Interviewer

I'll I thought we could start by talking a bit about your first book, *My Body Is a Book of Rules*. What struck me most about the book was how effectively you manage to incorporate all these different 'non-literary' forms—the academic essay, the screenplay, advice columns, psychiatrists' notes, and so forth—into your writing, capturing the essence of these different styles while still maintaining your distinct and consistent voice. How did you arrive at this style?

Washuta

I started writing this way when I was starting graduate school. I came in as a fiction writer, but my first quarter I was taking a non-fiction class and I really took to it, and really lost interest in fiction. So from the outset I was writing these essays that were 'weird,' you know—I started writing a chapter of the book during my first quarter.

David Shields was my professor, and he was bringing a lot of essays into the class that were in forms that I had never imagined before, and I was energized to get working on essays that were like that. My head just cracked open. I had all of this stuff in it, all these ideas, but also questions—what if I do this, what if I do that, will I be violating copyright, will I run into these kind of logistical problems—and David just said "do it, just do it, worry about that later, or never." I realize now that this is how I look at the world in general; I make comparisons between my experience and pop culture items, or forms I see in the world. And I think they always have, but now I can bring it to my writing. I go to the drugstore and I get that prescribing information and instead of throwing it out like I always did, one day I just looked at it and thought, right, this is a literary form—and I can use this in my personal nonfiction. For a while I was trying to force myself to write fiction that was recognizable as being like what I had studied during undergraduate years, and I appreciate that sort of traditional fiction approach, but it's just not something I'm good at.

Interviewer

Do you see that sense of experimentation, that willingness to do something different, as being particularly strong in the Northwest?

I never thought of it as being specific to this region, although it seems that people have been really receptive to what I do here. When I was trying to find an agent, then a publisher for the book, it was a bit hard, partly because they didn't know how they were going to sell it—but here, it always seemed obvious to me that readers were interested in my work and curious about it.

Interviewer

From the first lines of *My Body Is a Book of Rules*, you're locating yourself in both a physical place—the Northwest—and, by tracing your lineage back to Tumalth of the Cascade Indians, in a type of physical history. But as the book goes on, it becomes clear that your relationship with place and history is generally one of deep ambivalence. I think part of me was expecting the narrative arc to build up to you arriving in Seattle, settling in, and feeling in some sense at home—but that's not how it ends. You said in *Book of Rules* that 'you don't know why you still don't fit in' in Seattle. Now that you've lived here a little longer and found some success—your first book was selected as a finalist for the Washington State Book Award, you've published your second book with Portland's Future Tense—are you starting to feel more in place in the Northwest?

Washuta

I definitely am. I moved to Seattle when I was 22, and the book sort of ends at age 24—and I think by then I was starting to feel more at home in Seattle. I really took to Seattle quickly, I loved it from the beginning, but moving to Seattle was an act of escape. Similarly, I moved to Maryland from New Jersey to improve my life, my situation, by relocation. And when I moved from Maryland to Seattle, I realized that I was just trying to run away from my problems, but they weren't problems that were specific to Maryland. They were mental health problems and the trauma that I've written about in the book. Logically I knew that they wouldn't be resolved by moving, but I think that was a big part of choosing Seattle instead of choosing to stay in the D.C. area. I sort of thought that if I were to relocate myself I could hit the reset button on everything, and of course that wasn't the case. I've grown so fond of Seattle that I don't want to leave the area, and a large part of it is because of the writing community, but another part of it was resolving some of those problems—not completely, but resolving them more, to the point where I feel like my life is not the mess that it was when I had to constantly press the reset button.

Interviewer

What are some of the specific people and institutions in the community here that have stood out as important to you?

Washuta

I came to Seattle in 2007 to start an MFA program at the UW, and that program was super important to me. I learned so much there, I met such amazing people, both in my cohort and the professors, and I was so close with a lot of those people. They were just so influential to me as a writer. It was at the UW that I learned about the non-fiction that I had waiting inside me, that I just needed to find a way to put form to.

Then, while I was in grad school I started an internship at Hugo House, and that was a really formative place for me as well. I interned there, I volunteered there for long stretches of time, I ran the open mic for a while, I ran a series called 'In Print' that they used to have, I worked as their youth program coordinator, I had a fellowship there... I think that was where I really learned about literary community in a big way. I met so many people who modeled literary community for me, and I became really immersed.

And then, I have a pretty strong relationship with Elliot Bay Book Company. I've been to tons of readings there. My first outing in Seattle, the first time I really ventured outside my apartment to somewhere I didn't

"Bluffs Along Columbia River." Date Unknown.
OSU Special Collections.

know, was to go down to Elliot Bay when it was still in Pioneer Square. And it was scary, I didn't even know how to take the bus—but I just really wanted to do it. It's been important to me ever since, they've been so supportive of my work, and just so great in introducing me to new books.

There are so many more—Artist Trust, Lit Crawl Seattle, all the independent bookstores who have sold me books, literary magazines and other publications.

Interviewer

I loved all the pop culture material in *Book of Rules*. (As is typical for a Seattle guy, I particularly liked the segments on Kurt Cobain.) You write compellingly about the changes Seattle has undergone since that period— "Seattle's flannel soft focus has sharpened, the film has lifted"—and I was curious if you could talk more about how you see Seattle today, after these changes. How does it compare with the expectations you had about the city as a child, growing up during that time?

Washuta

I was slightly familiar with Seattle when I was a kid, because my Mom's twin lives here and we would come to visit every other year. So I knew that I really loved the evergreens, and I loved the water. I had all these natural things that I loved about the city, and those things lingered in my mind for a long time, and when I got here, there was no sense of letdown, there was no sense that what I remembered was more vivid or more pleasing than what I experienced. I came back and I felt like the natural world pieces of Seattle were in place as I remembered them. And, I think I had expectations that there would always be something happening that I could tap into. Growing up in a pretty rural area of New Jersey, I just really wanted to be somewhere where something was happening all the time. I wanted to be in the city, and Seattle definitely didn't disappoint in that way. When I got here there was always something going on, and I was always doing something, whether I was going out with friends or going to shows or going to readings. Any time I wanted to do something I could, and that was just exactly what I had been hoping for.

Now, I've moved out of the city, and I don't get in as much. I think I've had my fill of that—certainly of "nightlife"—and I've had my several years of tapping into that busyness of Seattle and that excitement.

Interviewer

Continuing on *Book of Rules*, I wanted to ask specifically about the Cascade Autobiography section, which functions as the narrative center of the book—it's the one section that's spread out throughout the other chapters. But, read as one piece, it could also be seen as one of the more traditional sections in terms of style. How did you come to this form for the Autobiography?

Washuta

That was a challenge, but there was an interesting opportunity there. As I went through the process of shifting chapters around and trying to find the overall structure for the book, that chapter presented the biggest challenge, because it seemed like it needed to be at the beginning, and at the middle, and at the end—it had to be everywhere. I was working with Nicelle Davis, who is a poet and my editor for the book at Red Hen Press, and she had the amazing idea to split it up. She did the splitting, and showed me where she thought it should go, and it worked beautifully. It was exactly what needed to happen, because I do think it's the backbone of the book in a lot of ways, and making it into pieces that are inter-chapters actually let it function that way.

Interviewer

In general, there's such an obsessive quality to the book... partially this ties to the types of writing you're playing with, but clearly you also have an intense personal relationship to questions of categorization, organization, definition. And that carries into *Starvation Mode*, too, which is literally presented (at least in Part 1) as a list of rules. Generally, I tend to think of 'rules' as oppressive, and limiting; yet, you're using this mode as a tool to understand your body, to make connections between seemingly disparate things, and to express yourself in a deeply personal way. How do you see this complexity playing out, these different forces coming together?

Washuta

I think I have a personality or temperament that's obsessive and responds well to clearly defined limits, and yet, there's also this strongly intuitive part of me. I gravitate towards unexplained things, and unexplainable things. I think in some ways when these sides come together, there's an interesting tension—between the wild part, that's a little bit boundless and intense, and these self-imposed rules that I have in so many parts of my life. I respond well to those rules at some times, and at other times I find them absolutely impossible to adhere to.

That comes out in my writing: there needs to be some kind of tension in any kind of work that I do, and some kind of conflict, but the conflict isn't the same as it would be in a linear, chronological book, with an 'arc.' There are plot points, but it's not really the same set-up, there's not suspense in the same way, like "what's gonna happen next." I just tell it all the beginning of the book. I think the tension there is the internal tension, between what I am and what I think I should be.

Interviewer

That's certainly how I saw one of the central tensions of *Book of Rules*—trying to balance this desire for sureness and certainty and clarity with a real concern about the restrictions those things carry with them. In a way, this reminded me of the whole idea of blood quantum, which, while problematic for a huge number of reasons, also seems to persist as a major part

"The Glaciers of Mount Tacoma" from *The Great Northwest*.
1883. Harold B. Lee Library.

of tribal identity and categorization. What's your impression of that sort of categorization, that form of definition?

Washuta

I think there has been a movement away from blood quantum among some tribes, and I'm really excited to see that. My tribe doesn't use blood quantum in determining membership, and there are some other tribes that don't, and I think of that as progressive enrollment policy—to make that movement away.

Since there are more than 500 tribes that are federally recognized, and more that are state-recognized or unrecognized, there's so many different ways of being a community member. For people who are unfamiliar with the complexities of Native identity and tribal membership, it can be easier to just look at a number, look at blood quantum, and use that to decide how "authentic" someone is. I think it can too often be a way of explaining someone away—of putting someone into a very small box, or set of boxes, so that native people can be "understood" and dismissed. If non-native people are able to look at native people and decide that some of us are not legitimate because we're not of an acceptable blood quantum, then they're able to uphold this ongoing genocide by deciding that a lot of us aren't really Indian, don't really exist. It cuts down on the number, in people's minds, of how many "real Indians" there are out there. Blood quantum has been written into U.S. law. It's functioned as a tool of government assimilation efforts, and it's no accident that it's shaped Americans' understanding of what it means to be Native.

Interviewer

Absolutely. Now, I wanted to talk more directly about your second book, *Starvation Mode*. How did that book come about?

Instant Future generally publishes books that are between 10,000 and 12,000 words, so I was writing something to try to fit into that length and format. I knew that I couldn't do things that were as weird on the page as I did in *My Body Is a Book of Rules* because I knew from the process of having that turn into an eBook that some of the formal elements are hard to replicate in eBook form—I could still experiment, but it would be a different kind of experimentation.

I had a couple of failed attempts at writing something, but eventually I decided that I wanted to write about my life's history of eating. My first book takes up so many different issues and so many different problems, and I thought it might be interesting to narrow it down into a single problem. I let some of the other problems come in, but really I wanted it to be focused on disordered eating, because I had not explored that as much as I thought I could.

I think I was also fueled somewhat by something somebody said in a review... somebody was frustrated by my unapologetic depiction of my self-loathing and fear of being fat when I had an eating disorder. And I really wanted to push back against that, because I won't apologize for that, for things that sprung from mental illness and were beyond my control. I was trying to be as honest as I could about things that were really eating at me, and the terror that I was experiencing. I wasn't going to sugar coat anything in the book. What I could do was explore those thoughts more deeply and show people just how hard it was to have an eating disorder— to have many forms of disordered eating over the course of my life—and to be even more unapologetic about how horrible that self-loathing feels and to be really explicit about exactly what it was.

Interviewer

How have you felt about the experience of releasing Starvation Mode as an eBook, specifically?

I think it's been really neat. It was so gratifying to have it come out so quickly. The first book took seven years to write and publish, total, and the writing and publication of *Starvation Mode* happened in under a year. After I was done with the final draft, it came out just a few months later. It's neat that readers were able to get it instantly on the day it came out. Anyone who wanted it, anyone who still wants it, can order it and receive it instantly. It was nice to be able to write something that was substantial and meaningful, but without going through the very long process of writing a book that was 60,000 words.

My editor at Instant Future, Matthew Simmons, is really great to work with, and the other authors who have released books on Instant Future (Litsa Dremousis and Zach Ellis) are excellent writers, really great people, and it's fun to be a part of that community.

Interviewer

I would imagine so—they're certainly doing fabulous work. Have you started work on your next project yet?

Washuta

Yeah, I'm working on my third book. It's going to be an essay collection, and it involves a lot of research; I have a few of the essays written, and a lot of them are ideas at this point. It's really going to focus on Indigenous identity, specifically my Cowlitz and Cascade identity, and I'm bringing in some stuff about pop culture and how pop culture warped my sense of who I am as a native person when I was growing up. There's going to be a lot in there about hauntings. There will be a few essays that are in unusual forms, and others that are not. I've gotten a lot more comfortable with writing essays that don't take the form of some weird document, but I still like to do that and am going to keep doing that.

It sounds like this book will also draw a lot from the Northwest. At this point, do you see yourself as, or do you call yourself, a 'Northwest writer?'

Washuta

I do. When I was in New Jersey and Maryland, I was only just starting to form as a writer. I was still just learning, not really creating things that were going to be published, for the most part, and still honing my craft. I feel like it was in the Northwest that I really learned how to write about myself—I learned where I fit into the literary world that I saw around me. Also, I'm from a Northwest tribe, and I think of myself as being from the Northwest for that reason, but I'm also from New Jersey. I'm from two places.

When I go down the street in the morning I can smell the Sound, and the trees here are huge, Richmond Beach is a few minutes away, Edmonds Beach is a few minutes away, and the views of the mountains here… when I first moved here, I was just mesmerized by the mountains, and it's never stopped. In Edmonds, I can see the mountains clearly and often, and every time I see those mountains—it just does something to me.

Interviewer

Do you see yourself staying around the area for the foreseeable future?

Washuta

I do. I've thought about the possibility of relocating, but I find it really hard to imagine not living here. I really appreciate being in Coast Salish territory and not being far from my tribe—that makes it really feel like home, at a very deep visceral level. And I have a lot of family out here, though my parents, brother, grandma, and other family members are still back east. But I think part of it is the literary community. I know that if I moved to another major metropolitan area I would be able to find a large community there, but it wouldn't be the same community.

There's other things about this area that are harder to explain, that I can't really put in list format. I feel really right in the environment of the Seattle area. The trees, the smell, the arrival of the seasons… they feel like what I was always meant to be living around, and going back east I see how I wasn't really in harmony with the environment I grew up with. The leaves falling off the trees in the winter and having bare limbs, the snow, the timing of the seasons just didn't feel right to me, and it feels right here.

—<o>—

This is Meant to Hurt You

Leah Sottile

1. Sick

En Media Res.

It is August and it is hot and in the other room my husband is dying.

It has become the only explanation that makes any sense. Joe is a 34-year-old man in constant, unbearable, searing-hot pain, a patient doctors have called a "mystery," as if that were some kind of comfort. The life he wants to live—where he's a graphic designer and a drummer—dangles in front of him. If he lives that life, he gets sick. If he doesn't...

He lies on our king-sized bed, his bare legs twisted up in the thin white summer sheets patterned with red branches and petals that look like droplets of blood. When he is awake, he shifts and writhes in constant misery, two box fans blowing hot air at his face. He sighs when things are bearable; he moans the rest of the time. He takes pain pills and suffers in the hot, dark room staring into the ceiling, past another fan whirring so fast its glass light fixture jiggles and plinks from the motion. He crawls to the bathroom.

It's a 100 degree day in our fourth floor west-facing apartment in a building made of brick. Our place is a pod of three small rooms—nothing fancy, but fairly new. From the win-dows, though, there's an unobstructed view of Portland's emerald green St John's Bridge. Its red lights blink from the tips of the bridge's spires day and night like slow-beating electric hearts. When we signed the lease on this place—in a brief moment of health—we reveled at the idea of the gothic gem of the Rose City outside our window, as if this would be our very own *Frasier* apartment.

But too many times lately, as we watch cop cars and ambulances fly over the bridge, sirens screaming, I worry about how close it is. What if, like the people we've seen teeter on the edge there, Joe, too, would feel the pull of the bridge's platform? What if after all these years of fighting he would shuffle out there in his pajamas and give up trying to figure out what was wrong with him? If anything was wrong with him?

Or what if it would be me out on the ledge there, the air whipping around me on a hot summer day?

Cool, quiet relief, for a moment. And then nothing.

2. Pain

February 2015.

It has been seven years since Joe first set foot in a doctor's office. Seven years of pills and syringes and ER trips, of visits to specialists who gave him a diagnosis of a disease we couldn't pronounce and no one we knew had ever heard of.

Ankylosing Spondylitis. It sounds like the scientific name of a dinosaur.

It is an awful biological creation, a mutation of the body that is sometimes called "bamboo spine" for how the backbone fuses into a hard, inflexible branch over enough time. For Joe to feel any semblance of a normal life, he sits for hours in a chemo center, surrounded by people with shaved heads and in wheelchairs, where the only drugs that make him feel better are administered through an IV.

"You don't have cancer, babe," I reminded him the first time we arrived for his treatment. "Don't start to think that way. You're not like these people. You're sick, but you're not dying."

Like every medication he'd tried before, these drugs worked for just long enough that life, it seemed, was normalizing. Joe was playing his drums in a band, even going on weekend-long Northwest tours. He was working. It started to feel like we were a normal couple in their early 30s again.

We planned a cross-state move. Joe took a new job with a big company.

It felt like we were finally strapping lead weights onto the memories of this past seven years, this time of misery and struggle and uncertainty, and we were watching it disappear un-derwater, sinking slowly toward the bottom of the ocean.

April 2015.

I don't know exactly when Joe's pain made its grand, dramatic reentry.

It starts in his neck: a hot pain that pulls his shoulder muscles tight like stiff ropes, that sends electricity up into his head and through his forehead, tightening like a vise around his skull. The word headache really doesn't do it justice.

The throbbing moves down his spine, into his lower back, bending him forward into a hunch, as if someone has smacked him across the back with a two-by-four and he's frozen there, unable to ever recoil from the blow.

But the worst of it is in his hips: a stabbing so miserable that he walks with a limp. Not like a bounce-walk after you've stubbed your toe: Joe's legs move like he is constantly trying to step onto a stair and missing every time. Calling it a shuffle would be too graceful: Joe walks like a lurching skeleton, a machine without grease. At doctor's offices and hospitals, he refuses wheelchairs from nurses who look at him with furrowed brows, preferring to be seen hobbling violently and slowly than to drop into the invisible, unseen realm of the wheelchair-bound.

He moves like a young man who has grown old overnight.

His mind is demolished as he comes to grips that there is no real reason why he's here. Why he's walking like this, or why he, a young man, has spent hours in waiting rooms beside women with white permed hair and men with canes while everyone else his age seems to be traveling the world and having children and buying houses.

There is no better way to explain it than this: shit happens.

Too many times Joe looks at me with those blue eyes I fell in love with so long ago. They're clear and desperate and angry. He asks me if he's crazy. If he feels so much pain, why can't doctors stop it? Is it all in his head?

"Of course it isn't in your head, babe," I say, because I can't tell him I've been wonder-ing the same thing all along. When you love someone, there are certain things you just can't say.

May 2015.

The doctor waits until after six to call, and when she does, Joe picks it up on the first ring.

She tells Joe that she's reviewed his MRI, and can definitively say that he's spent seven years treating a disease that she, an expert, does not believe he actually has.

This is good news.

This, to Joe, is bad news.

He is pissed. Fuming. Spewing *who-is-she-to-tell-me-what-I-haves*.

And I say maybe it's good news. Maybe this seven years of toiling was for nothing, and we can put it behind us.

And he looks at me again with those eyes and says he's still in pain.

That he's more scared now than he's ever been.

If his pain isn't caused by the disease he thought he had, he says, "Then what the fuck do I have?"

3. Blood

December 2003.

Joe's band was called These Arms Are Snakes.

They were a band for which fans were not casual, whose love ran so deep and true that many a young girl tattooed a black raven with an exposed red heart—the band's logo—onto their skin.

These Arms Are Snakes would become one of most popular underground punk groups in the country, signed to a respected independent label. They were strange and aggressive, sensitive and off-kilter. Joe, the band's original drummer, hit his drums with a ferocity and force that inspired just as many onlookers as the band's enigmatic lead singer. He pounded and pummeled: a beautiful, masculine violence.

But rock bands don't last forever. Joe knew he had more inside of him than just music, and he quit the band after two years of touring the country nonstop.

After his very last show in Seattle, he packed his forest green kit into their bright blue cases and piled into a 15-passenger van headed toward Spokane, his hometown, five hours to the east.

Less than an hour from his family's front door, the van hit a patch of black ice that caused the vehicle to spin out of control, slam into the guardrail on the right side of the road, whirl in a circle and, suddenly, stop. They were facing the wrong way, looking through the night mist at the approaching headlights of a semi-truck.

Joe was in the back, asleep across the middle bench seat without a seatbelt on. The sudden jerk of the van, set off it's smooth course, caused him to open his eyes and see the headlights bearing down on them, blinding and clear as if they were the eyes of God, and he thought to himself, "So, this is how it ends."

The truck, with a gargantuan piece of metal strapped to its open bed, jack-knifed as it steered and skidded to avoid the van, causing that hulking object to launch into the air and embed itself in the icy blacktop like a meteor.

When the truck collided with the van, the metal encasing left Joe and his friends crumpled and folded as if it were an empty soda can. The windows exploded, sending shards of glass into their hair and skin. There was a six pack of beer somewhere in the van, and the pieces pierced the tin spraying the terrified passengers in alcohol. One of Joe's drum cases launched into the head of one of his friends.

They were bloody and they were covered in beer, but the impact, somehow, didn't kill them. Everyone in the van, including Joe, walked away from it. The accident made the headlines of punk news sites.

For Joe, though, it was more than a Buddy Holly moment. As he stood there on the side of the freeway in the freezing cold, as ambulances and police cars swarmed around he and his friends, Joe knew that everything could have just ended. He felt lucky.

He had no idea that, somewhere deep inside his body, everything had just changed.

March 2004.

Joe was wearing freshly-pressed pants and a smart sweater when he walked into the newspaper office where I worked as a music critic. He wore cologne and had combed his hair. We met at the bottom of the spiral staircase that ran like a spine through the center of the office and I remember thinking he looked like a square.

He was smart enough to realize that people make a lot of assumptions about folks that look like he does, and he projected the very image he hoped would get him hired. Nice guy. Smart and easy to talk to. He got the job.

After a few weeks of winning the office over, Joe showed who he was. He grew out his beard, long and bushy and bright red. He arrived at work in jeans and t-shirts, revealing bright blue roses and a dead man in a gas mask tattooed across his arms. And he came upstairs, knocked on my cubicle wall and asked if we could get coffee and talk about music.

I said I had a boyfriend. He didn't care.

Soon I didn't either.

Before I met Joe, my world was a blur of beer-bottle green. My best girlfriends were the types who'd hold each others' hair back every weekend, but we never once talked about if we drank too much. We knew we did. I think we probably all silently agreed that we were having too much fun to overthink it. We were young, we had our whole lives to be sober.

My boyfriend back then was this Friday Night molotov: a corporate guy by day who was quick to throw fists on the weekend. I'll never forget dragging him away from a fistfight that tumbled out the front doors of a bar on Seattle's Capitol Hill. He'd starting something with a red-headed guy who looked at him wrong. It was embarrassing to be that girl clutching her purse with one hand and dragging her idiot boyfriend by the shirt out of a pile of bloody noses and split lips with the other.

But anger had always been attractive to me. It was never something I feared — just something I excused as a natural consequence of passionate people. In the house I shared with my friends, I covered the walls of my bedroom in portraits of it: pictures of WTO protests in Seattle, where anarchists covered their faces with handkerchiefs when cops used tear gas. Above my bed, amid punk posters and snapshots from protests I'd organized with my friends, there was a shot of Trent Reznor from Nine Inch Nails' "Head Like a Hole" video, dreadlocks flying as he's screaming into a microphone. There was a lot about the world that pissed me off when I was young, but I found an outlet for it through the punk and metal scenes. Anger, there, wasn't a scary thing; it was a shared human experience. Through our collective rage, we could disappear into the noise and feel more alive.

Not long after I met Joe, I knew my already-rocky relationship was done for when my ex said he liked Joe because he relieved him of needing to talk to me about music—as if it was this silly, passing thing I was nagging him with. I knew long before that Joe—who was broke then, living in his parents' basement— could give me more than that guy ever could. He wasn't an angry person. He was patient, quiet—a simmer to my inferno.

In an act of post-1990s courtship, Joe gave me some of his band's music to listen to. I would put in my headphones and play one of the songs on repeat as I walked to work. It's called "Drinking From the Necks of the Ones You Love." At the song's climax, the singer repeats these lines:

> *Tell the future to come in the back door,*
> *Tell all the stars that the stars are no more.*
> *Tell the future to come in the back door,*
> *Tell all the stars that the stars are no more.*

It's mumbling that turns, soon, to screaming. He says it again and again and again, Joe's drums rolling like a soldier's march behind the words and then everything explodes—the kind of rock and roll A-bomb that makes fans weak in the knees.

I listened to it over and over until I could feel those words driving my pulse, felt them pushing my heart into a steady beat and infusing the blood in my veins with a message: the future was Joe. If I let him in the back door of my life and waved goodbye to everything else I knew out the front, that the even the beauty of the stars, as I knew them, would change.

I remember when all was said and done, when months later we had an apartment together, we agreed that one day we'd have a good story to tell about our earliest days.

We didn't know then about the invisible darkness growing inside of

Joe. But it was as if his body did. As if it led him to quit the band he loved, guided him to find someone to help weather the storm that lay ahead, tumbling toward him like boulders of black thunderclouds.

To find someone whose neck he could drink from when the stars were no more.

4. Love

Late 2015.

You can say "in sickness and in health" all you want when you're 25 and standing at an altar, but really, are you picturing your loved one withering before you? Are you thinking of the lonely hopelessness that you'll feel when you offer your beloved their pain pills?

I wasn't. I thought I had my whole life to prepare for the "sickness" part of that statement. I was young and naive enough to believe that getting sick is only for old people.

It has been months since Joe got the call that he was misdiagnosed, an opinion that a handful of other doctors we visited agreed with. He goes to new doctors: rheumatologists, neurologists, pain specialists, speech therapists, physical therapists, occupational therapists and a pain therapist who explains to Joe what happens to the brain when the body hurts.

You panic.

We rule out diabetes, multiple sclerosis, cancer, low vitamin D levels, rheumatoid arthritis, lupus, Lyme Disease, cancer.

During a test to cross muscular dystrophy of the list, Joe lays on a bed in his underwear, and a lab tech inserts long needles into his muscles and twists a dial on an ancient looking computer, sending surges of electricity into his muscles. Joe winces in pain as the test progresses, his body jiggling. I pretend to look down at my phone. I don't want him to see that I'm crying.

When Joe goes on disability, suddenly we are together more than we ever have been, crammed in our hot apartment together.

I escape long enough to feel sane, but not long enough for Joe to feel abandoned. I put a leash on our dog and walk across our neighborhood toward a purple and yellow painted house with a coffee can stationed in front, the words "positive affirmation bucket—take one!" written in black marker across the top.

Day after day, I reach inside and pull out neon green slips of paper with hippie wisdom written on them. As much as I want to laugh at the idea of positivity coming from a coffee can, I cling to my pilgrimages here. I hope that one day the answer to surviving this time will be written on a slip of paper inside. On one visit, I think of upending the whole can, dumping all the affirmations onto the sidewalk and pawing through them until I find the one I need.

I am paralyzed by the guilt that I feel for being angry at Joe when he sends me links to ar-ticles called "15 Things Not to Say to Someone With a Chronic or Invisible Illness." I'm bitter at the minefield his body has set up for us to live in. I feel like I'm not married to just Joe, but to his illness, too—and I'm mourning seven years of my own life lost, as if he were this vampire sleeping beside me, draining my energy and drinking my blood in order to keep going.

And I feel so selfish for feeling all of it, for grieving a past that never was.

There are times when I cannot physically listen to Joe moan any-more—when I walk into the other half of the apartment, out of his sight, clap my hands over my ears and stretch my mouth wide in a silent scream.

One day, Joe interrupts me while I'm writing, cracking open the door to say "I love you?" A question, not a statement.

"OK," I say. He opens the door wider and tells me he can see how I look at him when he walks into a room. He can tell I dread the sight of him.

I tell him how I hate his disease, but I hate even more when he says he loves me like it's a question.

"If I didn't love you," I say. "I wouldn't be here."

*

In November, Joe gets a name for the way he feels. It's called fibromyalgia—a disease that doc-tors say many in the medical field don't actually believe is a real. They call it an invisible illness.

When we ask how he got it, doctors run down a list of potential triggers, several of which Joe had experienced.

"Have you ever been in a bad car accident?" one asks, and Joe and I look at each other, a photograph of the crumpled van so many years back flashing across the movie screen in my mind.

For some people, a traumatic event like that is something they shake off. Maybe they go through physical therapy for a while, or they take pain pills. But for others, like Joe, their bodies become a written record of their past, aching and creaking in such a way to remind them of how quick, how fragile and how fast this life is.

*

By 2016, Joe's body starts working again. He can walk, he starts to work. He leaves the house everyday and suddenly—just as fast as he got sick—life becomes normal. Quiet.

We move, too, out of the apartment that became the stage for the worst of his sickness. We get a house in the country where an ostentation of peacocks struts across the lawn, fanning their feathers and standing on our fenceposts to crow at the sky. At night the old tree by the bedroom creaks and a wooden chicken coop door slams and groans in the wind.

One of the first nights after we moved in, I looked out the bathroom window. It was black outside, not a light around except the stars. A heavy wind was stirring, and the bamboo chimes I'd hung out on the porch were chattering in bursts. It wasn't quiet, but it was peaceful, and it occurred to me that I couldn't recall a single time in the last decade when I had used that word to describe my life.

We sat down to eat dinner recently and Joe stopped me when I referred to a period of time as "back when you were sick"—as if it were some kind of ancient history.

"I'm still sick," he said. "I'll always be sick."

It hadn't occurred to me that even before Joe was in pain, he was sick. That when he asked me to marry him in our kitchen as I was cooking dinner one night, he had been sick then, too. He just didn't know it yet.

There were times throughout the worst of Joe's pain when I sobbed uncontrollably about this horrible hand we'd been dealt. The thing I remember about those times is how much worse it made me feel to cry on the shoulder of a sick person.

But that is what love is. It is a thing defined at the worst moments of our lives. Love happens at the bottom, when we willingly tilt our necks to the sides, push our hair away from our neck and offer up our own arteries to drink from when there is no other way to take the pain away.

—<o>—

A Multiplicity of Gray

Monet P. Thomas

"Her focus on works in palettes of white, black and a multiplicity of grays could not appear more dramatic nestled in the ivory bays and continuously flowing spirals of the Guggenheim's interior."

—Michael Fitzgerald, *The Wall Street Journal*

I should've been in Philadelphia, not queued outside the Guggenheim with A-. On exhibit: *Picasso in Black and White*. Just after Christmas, in the throwaway days of December, we should not have been together. Not that way. Now, years later, this day feels made up, ridiculous. I don't want to believe I could be unfaithful, that I chose to be unfaithful. But the day did happen. Standing there in the line, the morning so cold in the city, my body shook. And A-, visiting home from Spokane, was so close that the air between our bodies was warm.

The truth is, parts of that day I engineered: making him pick me up for bagels and coffee, the ride into the city. Other parts were chance: how we got lost, realizing I wasn't going to make the bus to Philly even as we sped toward it. I should've said, *A-, take me home*. I'd wanted a few moments with him, I admit, but I didn't expect a whole day. We didn't know about Picasso. We just saw the iconic white building against the sleet sky, decided *Why not?*

It took Frank Lloyd Wright years to complete the blueprints for the Guggenheim, after countless revisions and fights with the patron. He would never see the physical manifestation of his work before his death. Before the Guggenheim, just about all museums and art galleries used an open design, consisting of a series of interconnected rooms, which forced participants to retrace their steps and experience the art a second time as they exited. Wright's original vision, utilizing a sloping ramp and an elevator, directly contradicted that model. Using the elevator, museumgoers would begin at the top of the gallery and follow the downward momentum of the ramp, engaging with the art in a uniform and linear experience.

Standing in the lobby and looking up at the winding bays, the skylight, I couldn't help but think Wright accomplished even more than he aspired to. The structure was overwhelming and church-like in its dignity. I felt the urge to pray, though I never prayed. I had to tell myself, "You are not a tourist. Close your open mouth." But like tourists, ignorant of our ignorance, we started up the ramp, not understanding why there was a line for the elevator.

"You feel art and architecture converging as you turn from the daring yet delicate spatial enigmas in The Accordionist (1911), one of the grandest of all Picasso's Cubist compositions, to the shifting spatial arabesques that are revealed all through Wright's mobius strip of a museum."
—Jed Perl, *The New Republic*

I knew next to nothing about Picasso prior to our trip to the Guggenheim. I knew the artist was Spanish, had seen pictures of *Guernica* and knew vaguely of its implications. My explanation of Cubism would've involved hand motions as well as words. And I knew that, like Wright, much of Picasso's mythos was tied to his numerous affairs. Standing behind A-, who always got as close as the crowd and security allowed, I looked past him, tall and thin, and saw what books and lectures couldn't teach me. Art should stand like a building or a child grown to be an adult—without help or explanation, without preamble or backstory. Even as I try to tell you about this day, I can't know if I'm telling it right.

Up and up we went, the crowd growing as the lunch hour neared. I followed close on A-'s heels, but didn't hold his hand, though I wanted to with everything inside me. Instead, I held onto the dark hem of his winter coat as his height and determination parted the crowd. The biggest group formed in front of a section of *Guernica* in monochrome, the artist's draft before the famous version. The horse's head in white with box teeth. Black shapes of space, an open gray mouth.

"Interesting," A- said.

"I think I like it in color better." I said.

"Yes," said A-, said, "but look how many shades of gray there are."

I looked. We moved on. I'd always thought of Picasso in riotous color, but over and over we saw he'd found infinity with just black, white, and gray. And despite the reviews I'd read later, I still saw Picasso's women: his daughter, his wife, his mistress, his other mistress, his muses. He could never be without them.

"Black and white intensifies our sense of Picasso's changeableness. You see black as line and plane, surface and substance, pure thought and pure emotion."
—Jed Perl, *The New Republic*

I know what it means to be changeable. I'd changed my mind about what was more important to me more than once, but in the end I went with knowing there would always be food on the table. I didn't know if I could be an artist without a muse, but I knew I couldn't be an artist at all if I was starving.

The night A- finally kissed me, we were standing outside my Spokane apartment building, the night air cooling around us. Summer was slowly giving way to autumn. I'd be gone in a week. Even now, I can feel his hands on my body: one on my face, the other gripping my side, like he'd been waiting his whole life. I kissed him back. I already loved him. I didn't want to use those words then, but it was love filtered through a multiplicity of gray, closer to black than white, and not enough.

"The spiral layout, affording generous views ahead and behind, might actually be the perfect format for Picasso displays. The artist, after all, was always looking back at himself even as his creative drive corkscrewed ahead. The theme-and-variation dynamic that emerges establishes not just the high level but the true nature of Picasso's intelligence."

—Sebastian Smee, *Boston Globe*

The day at the Guggenheim was a stolen day. The last of its kind, and we knew. For us, sharing art was as much an act of infidelity as going to a hotel room. We didn't talk about the past, the other people in our lives. I was myself, in love, distant. He was himself, quiet, sure. We looked at the Picassos, shoulder to shoulder when space allowed, unfaithful together. At the top of the gallery we leaned forward against the railing and looked down. The lobby was swarming like a hive but without a seeming purpose. A woman in a trench coat had her head tilted back, looking up at the skylight, her straight black hair falling behind her.

We failed to fulfill Wright's vision—a clean path from elevator and ramp is rarely fully realized by the average museum-goer. But on reflection, I found the second viewing of the art instructive. I followed A- down, studied the line of his neck, and remembered how my mouth felt against that one soft place. I remembered the nights I knew I loved him, but would not pursue it, instead choosing to stay with who I was already with, the two of us quiet and content. I remembered the first day we met in a park. Down we went along the sloping ramp. It had been summer, and then was winter. The lobby came quickly, the ground flat again and then we were stepping out onto the street. It was snowing, the flakes melting when they touched the ground. The sky still, and light, and gray.

—◦—

Unplace

Chris McCann

Like birds through the trees

The blood was everywhere in the little room in Abumombazi. Spatters turned the concrete walls into ragged curtains, and the air hung heavy in the thick afternoon light.

She plunged into the man who would not stop bleeding, trying everything she knew to contain him. November and it was near 100 degrees, air so viscous she had to push it aside with both arms to move across the room.

Later, in the lull before dinnertime, she rubbed the blood and dirt and sweat deeper into her still-pale skin with a damp rag. As the dark fell like birds through the trees, she imagined for a moment the line between the sea and sky as the sun began to rise. On the coastal plains, she walked between the sea wrack and the gorse, squinting out toward the western horizon, waiting for the angle of the sun to illuminate the division between water and air.

Although she did not, would not, admit it to anyone later, she marked down the first day she began to cough, a dry, shaking thing that did not seem appropriate in this climate. Lacking her usual energy that Wednesday, she barred the door and sat inside the closet-sized room that held her bed. Past the wood slats of the window, she heard the first fat drops of rain hit the leaves of a banana tree, clattering around in the branches, and tumbling to the ground. Though her eyes were closed, she saw the puffs of dust rise up from the dirt, like holes in the body of the earth.

Too dark, she thought, and coughed. Soon she would leave. There was a part of her that understood, even though no one at that time could have said what it was, the thing that had begun to unravel her. Later, there would be tests and batteries of medication, flights where she would skim the earth to be examined, the bright lights of home, the engaging sea. In her nurse's arms, she would then subside, after all this, having not been able in the rush to even clean the walls of blood. Having not, in the end, been able to even save herself.

For now, though, she chewed carefully, tongue probing for the sharp chicken bones that sometimes made it into her moambé. The children no longer ran from her, and that, then—despite what came after—was what remained with her, long after she'd forgotten everything else. Their wide eyes, their silence.

In the north at that moment, the sea shone for a few hours at the end of the vanishing year, while down here in the forest, all the light was red.

Whose body?

Autumn leaves. A swirling cloud of carmine, pumpkin, ocher. *The thing was*, she thought, because she could not stop thinking. The thing was that the hard edges of the leaves, the brittle leaves, the ones that could not hang on in the latest wind, although it had not been overly strong—*how sad*, she thought, knowing that sadness really had nothing to do with it, nor did trying, nor did—but the edges, their small serrations. This one, in particular, because what was anything if not a single instance, a peculiarity even in the midst of sameness? She asked herself these questions, although she was not really asking herself anything. Instead, the voice that asked the questions came from somewhere else and did not expect any answers.

At this point, the phone rings and someone—her mother, she thinks—starts banging on the door. Or the window. The birds outside still sing, but she can tell that something is wrong. The ringing and ringing. The doorbell, a shattering of glass. She holds the leaf in her hand, tracing its edges with her own ragged fingernail. Because she is the singularity, or at least that's what the voice is saying over all the commotion that disturbs her but does not change the way the leaf seems to be singing.

And this tune—no words, of course—gives her the permission she hasn't asked for to rise and walk toward the back of the house. As she does, she feels arms like vines—or vines, like arms—attempt to hold her back, to slow her progress. It is like walking through seaweed, the slime on her arms and face and legs, the sucking noises. Still, she proceeds.

This is one of those times that she knows she is screaming, but she cannot hear herself. Like at the dentist when you smell the burning, but don't feel the drill. But she is the drill. She is always the drill.

In front of her, the forest looms, with more trees than she expected. She feels deceived, or the voice tells her she does, by the sheer number of things she has mistaken. *The leaf, though*, it says. Its edges. How it angles at the same time away toward the forest, toward the kitchen, toward the body. *Whose body?* Whose indeed.

Separated by a single—no, double—pane of glass from all these trees, she launches herself toward them, only to be pulled back by the vines, by the arms. Now she hears the screaming. As the leaf falls from between her fingers, she watches it drift toward the floor. Restrained, she feels its flight, the late light illuminating the borders between it and the air and her body as they continue, continue, continue to erode.

The effects of the human

The road just ends, like that. In nothing. In a field that is not a field at all. Instead, a landscape of harrowed orange-red mud, oozing toward the town.

And it is into this non-field that Guillermo walks, walks away from the last buildings, the house where nobody lives, the house where people go to disappear, the house with the curtains drawn.

His boots squelch in the mud. He trudges. And trudges. And still he is not far enough. The border, if that's what it is, lies at least another day's walk away, according to the people who've been there, and come back. A very small percentage, he remembers thinking, later, as he sits somewhere without a name, without the papers he never had to begin with.

But he does cross the line and then keeps walking as the mud becomes grass becomes fiery bushes bright with thorns becomes dust becomes stones. When he stops, it is in a small town called Lagarto, though there is no water for miles. The name, some old man chewing his tongue tells him, comes from the mine. *Are you here to work?*

Despite the endless hours of walking and sleeping in silence, in holes, in the declivities of the land, in the gullies, the ravaged valleys of the south, Guillermo has not yet had the opportunity to consider the answer to that question. Though *opportunity* might be the wrong word because it was that process of consideration precisely that he was walking away from when he left a small village he's already forgotten the name of.

The question, then. *Yes*, he says, believing it to be the most correct of any number of plausible answers. But the man shakes his head, glances darkly at the sky, and spits upon the ground, causing a small plume of dust to erupt from the surface of a stone, rise briefly, dissipate, and then fall, diminished. In moments, all trace of it is gone. *The effects of the human on an inhuman landscape*, Guillermo thinks, because he has not stopped analyzing that which lies outside his mind simply because he has left his home.

A ferric line of ants bars the ground, separating the two men's boots, Guillermo, and the man who could never be his father. *Best to move along*, the man says, but Guillermo's already walking away down a road that has recently been graded, small mounds of dirt and rocks at fairly regular intervals off to the side like mountain huts for small travelers. A bed, a cook stove with some gas, a small window. What else does the hiker need?

Companionship, perhaps, but he knows better than to expect a replacement for what he has so willfully left behind. Instead, the dun serpent wallowing in the gray dust. The dead lizard, desiccated, brittle. The new road, foundering unsurprisingly just 200 steps from where it began.

Something you can do to save yourself

The problem was that the board needed a hole. You could get a plastic seat and some chains at the hardware store, but if you wanted a wooden seat, you had to make it yourself. Which involved a drill that had a large enough bit and enough torque to do the job. Meaning, today, that this job would not get done.

Again. He feels the summer slipping away from him. Already, slipping. As in that moment when you're about to fall, but haven't hit the ground yet. When you believe, mistakenly, that there is something you can do to save yourself. The disparate parts of your body all searching for purchase when there is none to be found.

He stares out the window over the kitchen sink at the tree branch holding the rope. *Where is the swing that will entertain us?* the voices say. The voices echoing against the brittle chambers of his head. *Oh, where is the joy of summer, the elation of swinging free from the branch of the old oak tree?*

The coffee pot grumbles, the dishwasher chokes on something. All the windows that have been closed overnight now need to be opened. Again. The scent of the lawn, the birds. Those glorious, flitting birds. He cannot stop the plunge of the day to watch them, but he would if he could. Slow the whole damn thing to a slug's ooze and just stand and stare at those, he has no idea what they are—swifts? sparrows?—as they zing through the fragrant air like machines, brushing the very tips of the newly shorn grass with their bellies for what appears like the sheer fuck of it all. Those brilliant birds.

Perhaps he can borrow a drill. Perhaps he will need to retrench and admit that a plastic seat and chain will not cause the summer, this summer, to collapse around them all in despair. Indeed, the red plastic seat might seem almost jaunty in the sparkle of the early morning. With the birds—swifts, sparrows—darting among the various waves of light to stitch up the sky.

From its wounds. Because let's not kid ourselves, there are wounds and they will not just go away with the heady feeling of flight, transient though it may be. No, they will not go away with the kick of a foot off the spongy grass, but they may be lessened, they may be lightened. And at least it will be complete, that sweet arc from ground to sky and back to ground again. And back to sky. He drinks his beer amid the skimming of the birds, as all the humans, too, perform their practiced motions. Until—and here he finally catches the breath he's been chasing—the whole thing looks not unlike a great, silent machine run entirely on air.

A good, solid weight

She had been waiting for weeks and then all at once it was over. A dark, cloudy evening, the smoke in the air. At the tips of her fingers, she could tell that it was almost, but not quite, spring. At that point, which is why she and several others had chosen it, the Tuman was shallow with a sandy bottom, and slow moving. All she had to do was not get caught.

The brightest part of the night was the water, carrying a slick scum of industrial pollutants that gave it an orange sheen she wouldn't be able to fully shake for another few days. And the smell… something between diesel fuel and bubblegum, sweet and familiar.

On the other side, near a small graveyard town called Yueqingzhen, the others had people waiting for them, and so were quickly whisked away, cloaked in warm synthetic comforters dotted with cherry blossoms or smiling cats. She waited until the night had inhaled them all before rising from her crouch near the bank. Under a different sky, she walked away from town south toward Bailongdao, a town with nothing, she'd heard, to recommend it except a man who would take people to a slightly larger place called Tonghua, where, if you were lucky, you might be able to convince someone to bring you to Shenyang. And from there, well, she thought, she might as well be in Beijing.

She repeated these names to herself as she trudged through the mud and marshes that lined the river. With each step, they lost more and more meaning, becoming not places she would arrive, but talismans she felt clinking in her pockets, along with the modest amount of kuai she'd been able to collect using methods she'd not discuss with anyone.

Just like them all, she'd left a family and she still couldn't imagine any way to talk about that. She whispered *Chanxinping, Xiashijian, Zhongping, Heqitun, Bailongdao* to herself as she walked. It was so dark and desolate here, and the river murmured unceasingly, so she almost didn't see the man with the gun who was standing atop a small hill looking back across the river.

There was no question, however, of him not seeing her, backlit as she was by some great redness in the sky she imagined might be dawn. He turned his gun toward her and approached. Stricken, desperate, she couldn't move until he was just a few steps away at which point she threw herself down at his boots and began to pray.

He touched the barrel of the gun to her neck and prodded her up. He was Korean, she saw, but that meant nothing until he whispered that he, too, had crossed the river. That there were more of them coming and he was the lookout. She closed her eyes and imagined them lining up across the river, then wading in, what was it called? Baptizing themselves in the sickly waters, then washing up here, nowhere, having been reborn into, what did they say? The spirit.

She returned to her knees, not believing anything, but feeling, now, so tired. And not knowing what to do next, other than keep walking to connect the names of the towns she'd memorized. Which suddenly seemed like a stupid, hopeless thing to do.

Come with us, the man said. *Are you alone? We are going to Bailongdao.* Her heart leapt such as it never had. The pieces of her former life began to shine with all the reflected light that stayed inside her for fear of illuminating everything.

And that's when she knew he was lying. There were no others in the river waiting to be born again. Bailongdao was just some name on a map; it probably didn't even exist. She began to question whether the river she'd crossed was even the right one. Perhaps she was only halfway home, stuck in some isthmus of no country, unable to return or go on. She spat in the man's eye, and turned to run as he struck her with the butt of his rifle, knocking her down into the mud.

When she awoke, she was in a room made of glass. She'd had no choice. Anyone would have done the same. As she smiled for the tiny cameras that dotted the unbreakable windows like splattered bugs, she repeated her own name again and again, louder and louder until she was screaming it, but still nobody came.

Buy them all

The first mistake was the Greenpeace fair. I mean, up till then, we'd kept to ourselves, tight, like that. But then I wanted her to start thinking about the world, its problems, and do something, anything, to help. So I suggested the fundraiser, helped her make the signs and staple them to poles around town. Clunk, clunk, clunk, clunk, I can still hear the staples as they bedded in the wood.

It was one of those things, you think. That your kids should be exposed to. So that they understand. And she took the money she'd made on cookies and lemonade and selling some of her dolls and toy cars, and she counted it out and brought it to me in a box. I wrote the check and kicked in the stamp, and then, as far as I was concerned, it was done.

Good, and done.

But for her, it was just the beginning. Over the next few years, she emptied our house with fundraisers, even selling my records for Burma or Myanmar or wherever. Summers, she got internships and externships and handed books to my wife and me, that serious look in her eye, pressing our hands as she made the handoff, as she trusted us to allow this book, and the next and the next, to change our lives.

It turned out that I was too old for that, although she was successful with my wife, who left when she realized the extent of suffering going on in the world, *literally*, as she said, *literally under our noses*. On our watch. She disappeared into the trackless wilds not three years ago, and while I still receive postcards from places I never knew existed, they never say anything that I can understand.

My daughter, although she did not go then, has left recently, for good, I think and she says. *For good*. I believe her and force myself to be proud of her, although I wake every night gasping. Visions of her coming to me, blood streaming out of her eyes. Or lying on the ground covered in snakes. Or half-buried, clumps of dirt like rotting flowers in her hair.

Of course, these are just dreams. I sit here now, picking out words on a keyboard, waiting for her replies. She tells me about the markets there, how you can buy voodoo charms that will keep you alive forever. *Buy three*, I type, but she goes on to discuss the distribution of water and how there aren't enough clinics set up to allow the volunteer nurses and doctors to treat the sick.

Buy three, I type again. *Buy them all*. But she does not write back. The Internet goes out so often during our conversations that I'm not surprised, but I still sit here, sick, too, with no one coming to take care of me, no fetish dangling from my neck. While I watch the cursor blink, I see her there, in that yellow light, the dust from the east rough on her rough skin.

Sandpaper, she writes, as though she were here with me, listening. *A hammer and nails. A gun.* And I realize that someone else is with me, someone who is not my daughter, who, perhaps, has never been my daughter. There does not seem to be enough air in this room for me to catch my breath. I open a window, which helps a little, and then I type *goodbye* to that person who responds with a question mark, and the colon and parenthesis of a smile.

No withering, no death

Two hours outside the capital, there are no roads, only rivers. *There is no illusion. There is no cessation of illusion.* In the afternoon, the crumbling asphalt between road and no road steams. The encroaching greenery is making it nervous, because once one foot is lost, once one inch is reclaimed, then is it not only a matter of time until the capital itself, great city of dreams, is smothered in vines and given back to the river?

For three days, Gilbert's teeth have been aching, but he cannot afford to see a dentist, even the one who practices under the trees in the Garden of Palms. After work one day, he borrows a shovel from a friend and takes the bus to the Krikie Nigi camp where he will begin digging. It won't take much, and the ground is full of gold, or at least that's what they say, the Brazilians, the ones who stand too close and look too deeply into your eyes. The ones who have arrived in the night and say they will never return.

In moments, Gilbert is covered in sweat and mud. The others, up to their waists in pits of their own digging, seem to be having success, but he does not even know what to look for. He thinks they would tell him, but he's embarrassed to ask them, the bulging muscles of their arms, their hands full of shining mud.

There is no withering, no death, no end to withering and death. There-fore, he thinks, why am I not free of these aching teeth, this endless futile searching for relief, for rest? He feels something in the pit and thrusts his hands into the mud, scrabbling for a finger hold as though he were a doomed climber. Gold. It must be gold.

Up to his arms in mud, he realizes he is stuck. When he tries to pull his boot from the mud, his upper torso inclines further downward. *The body as a simple machine*, he thinks. Then, *fuck*. Now, his face is just inches above the muck, so even if he were to cry out, no one would hear. A new pain rushes into his ears and out his gasping mouth, stuck there with no one to help him, although he knows he has found something that will change his life.

With the sun gone, the red mud turns black. The sounds of the forest switch on, but he also hears the engines of trucks as they rumble back toward the city on that crumbling road. He struggles a bit, then begins to cry, but it is only when he has given up completely that four arms wrestle him out of the mud. He sits there, staring up into their headlamps. The streams of light muscle their way through the particulate darkness, glinting off the crudely shaped nugget of gold he holds in his dripping hands.

One of his saviors says something in a language he doesn't understand, then snatches the nugget before turning off his headlamp and striding away into the night. The other man hands him a small flashlight and then, too, turns away. As he begins the trudge back to the city, he notices that his tooth has ceased to ache. *There is no beginning to suffering, no end to suffering.*

In the night, the night birds sing for all the gold that is left in the ground.

The abdication of the subject

Ask anyone about it and they'll tell you that Rottumeroog is uninhabited. Has been since the vogt died in 1965. What they don't know is that Wilhelm has been building his bunker there since 2003. Bit of a hiccup when the island split in two back in 2012, but work progressed, after the requisite bit of soul searching.

As in, *why am I building this bunker here, a place that will surely be washed into the estuary before I die?* But, I argued, it was precisely the fact that it would be washed away, elided by the sea, that made it all worth doing.

Wilhelm has renounced his citizenship. German, originally, but now, he is nothing. He likes to say that he is himself, alone, but only under his breath when no one is listening. And I, well, you would say that I am Wilhelm's prisoner and have been since he abducted me from that Shell station outside of Maarssenbroek some seven years ago.

Although, as with everything in this country, it's a little more complicated than that. See, I was running away and was, to be completely honest, not averse to being abducted as long it took me far away from my village of K. A place that had grown odious to me. Exponentially with the years, with my deepening understanding. The red faces, the constant striving, the false cheer.

I welcomed the abduction, especially since Wilhelm is not your typical abductor. I should stop myself there. I don't have the breadth of experience to make that claim, having been abducted only once in my 34 years. *Once is enough*, Wilhelm always says, though not about that.

I think that if he knew I was as happy as I am, he might return me. There is that side of him that is fueled by unhappiness, his own as well as the misery of others. It's the reason he embarked upon this doomed experiment, and also why he's been so successful.

Because it is a success, at least for now. The bunker houses the two of us, protects us from the predatory seals and the occasional official who motors over to the island to reassure himself that it is still evolving. The mainlanders seem obsessed over the constant changes to the shape of the island. And there's a fair bit of self-congratulatory talk. As in: "The island has been largely left alone." Note the abdication of the subject. They are so laissez-faire that they're not even in the sentence.

Not Wilhelm and I. We are pioneers on these shifting sands. Beneath, actually, but let's not quibble over semantics. We come and go by night, under the power of no engine, no sail. We tread the seas together, captor and captive, both unnamed, unnamable. And what you understand of our lives together would fill a teaspoon, while we gaze over the water at your own doomed enterprises, comprehending the vast scale of your failure.

Still, I take no pleasure in unhappiness, even when it is that of my oppressors. Instead, I keep my eyes on the water. I model my life after the oystercatchers, those obvious and strident birds, as I nest in my own bare scrape, pebbles and sand—amid the constant wash of the sea.

It hurts

There was a time that he was on the island of Palau in the middle of the South Pacific. He couldn't remember now what had brought him there, but what he did was build cabinets to be installed in the houses that were being constructed. There were not many houses being constructed at the time he was there, but he built the cabinets for all of them. And he was a very careful carpenter, despite being young, probably too young to be so far from home.

He did not get homesick. He was not that kind. Instead, he focused on his work and he drank Red Rooster amber with the other men who worked for the contractor who built most of the homes on Palau. At the time, this contractor was quite upset that he had not received a recent contract to build a large waterfront home on a piece of property that was owned by a minor Hollywood actor. The carpenter told him not to worry about it, that he already controlled most of the construction and remodeling trade on the island.

Still, the man said. *It hurts.*

After a year, the carpenter began to feel restless and decided to return home. He met a woman at the grocery store and the two of them bought a small house together where they would grow old and die. The house had a front porch and some room in the back for a vegetable garden, although the carpenter did not particularly enjoy vegetables with the exception of fresh-shucked corn. He would eat as much corn as you would give him.

Despite the improvements that they made to the house, the woman realized that she no longer wanted to live there and so she left. The carpenter fixed a few things that had broken and then sold the house to a young family with a baby and two dogs. Since it was a small town, he met the new owners and told them about his time on Palau. He said he was thinking of going back there, although he knew he never would.

Instead, he drove to Alaska to work on the boats, but he had never enjoyed the sea and would often become sick. After he made enough money to justify the trip, he returned to the small town where he once owned a home. The house was still occupied by the young family and the carpenter saw that they now had another baby, but that one of the dogs had died. There was a small grave marker in the backyard, the place where his former wife had planted a row of cucumbers, several rows of peas and some kale.

During the days, he would drive by the house once or twice, just to see if the older child seemed to be happy playing in the front yard that he'd fenced. She did. But at night, he would park his car several blocks away and walk through the alleys until he reached the back fence and the gate that he'd fixed. It was fixed so well that he was able to open it without a sound and then walk slowly into the yard, sticking to the shadows made by the trees that had been there long before he'd bought the property.

He reached the grave of the dog where he would sit with his head in his hands, concentrating. The dog's spirit was still there, he could tell, and that reminded him of something he'd learned from the contractor in Palau. If a thing died and it was remembered too fondly, it could never move on to its rightful place in the other world. And the carpenter cried, then, for the dog and for the children and for his wife and for the contractor.

Outside the fence, the police were waiting, and he shook hands with the two officers before they escorted him to his car and followed him as he drove out of town, into the unincorporated lands of the county where the summer fires had already started to burn.

Under a small tent, not so long ago, a woman waits for a man. She drinks coffee from a small thermos and pages through a collection of poems saved from Mongols during the 13th-century destruction of Baghdad. As a girl, she had been taught that everything in the House of Wisdom had been destroyed by the invaders, but over the past 20 years she'd found perhaps a dozen books that had survived, spirited away by a conscientious scholar, tucked into a hole in an unmarked wall, buried in the sand.

The survivors were often missing parts of themselves, in this case the first few pages, so that it was difficult to identify the authors. But the names were not important, not anymore, not after so many years.

She sat halfway between the world and the rose garden of the poems, the mystical divan she felt she would never truly understand. She drank her coffee black although she gravitated closer to the dervish than the ascetic. And still, the man did not arrive.

He was a soldier and so her first thought was always of death, though there was no war now. And so she would walk herself back from the calamity of her soldier's death to an irritation with his lack of a sense of time. For he was always late, no matter the engagement, and reading medieval poetry under a small tent on the shores of a lake alive with fierce black flies, she had to admit, was probably not one of his favorite things. Still, he had said she could choose. During this time when he was not fighting, they'd agreed on that.

With a whisper of wild barley grass and a parting, briefly, of the cloud of flies, he arrived. She pushed herself into him, murmuring words we could not hear, not even with the microphones stationed at regular intervals around the small patch of land they occupied. And then began the interminable process of poetry, first one and then the other whispering the words to each other, pausing, looking out onto the flat, green waters of the lake, embracing, embracing again.

This stuff, while not illegal, should have been, and I kept the cameras rolling in the hopes that some future administration would see this effrontery for what it was—a kick in the teeth of all good people everywhere. It had to be said that the flies were getting worse, though they seemed to be leaving the lovers alone, and at one point I stumbled in trying to remove one from my ear. Stumbled and fell. And looked up into the barrel of a gun, for soldiers here, even when there is no fighting, do not forget to carry their weapons.

I had nothing to say, and so I began talking about the dissolution of the Abbasids and the nightingale and the rose. I showed, even there in that godforsaken place, that I was not unlearned. And the gun barrel slowly descended, leaving in its place the face of a man who watches sparrows.

Sitting together, under the small tent, I pointed out the placement of the microphones and showed them the video. We discussed the predicament of the inconstant beloved when presented with the fervent lover. While they, entwined like weeds, offered me sweet dates and pistachios in exchange for my promise of silence.

Some half-crazy dream

Hands shaking, perspiration dripping from his forehead onto the already slick keyboard, Dr. Bhagooli, senior lecturer at the University of Mauritius, amends the last few footnotes to his soon-to-be-published paper announcing the discovery of a new endemic species of the brown seaweed *Sargassum robillardii*. He stops to sip his sweating gin and tonic and grimaces as the bitter quinine hits the back of his throat like a needle.

Too late, he thinks, and then downs the rest of the drink. He's had malaria for 16 years, 11 months and 23 days, which is almost as long as he's been working with seaweed. The two facts of his life intertwined like an adolescent *Hypnea musciformis*, its cylindrical branches with their desperate tendril-like hooks. And in all likelihood attached to a hardy sargassum, the two plants and all their meanings coexisting forever in the warm, shallow seas of his imagination. *Time, my god, for another drink.*

Outside his small house in the sugarcane fields near Piton, Dr. Bhagooli listens to the humming of the mosquitoes as they zing through the heavy air. He's taken to leaving the windows open and has torn down the screens, which once protected the porch, because at this point, who cares. There's no saving him now.

Still, he's been intrigued lately by the research pointing to the ability of some varieties of the sargassum species to inhibit the *in vitro* growth of the malaria parasite. And although he has told no one, Dr. Bhagooli has established a small seaweed farm of his own just off the coast. The robillardii, of course, his now-adolescent child, the hope of his old age.

And when he drives down to the sea, it is in the dark of the night, when no one can see the tremors that rack his body, his constant stunned amazement in the face of an illness that cannot be cured. *Except*, he thinks, *through the studied application of years of research and an unhealthy willingness to toss it all away in the hope of some half-crazy dream.* He drives to the sea each night, because the plant must be fresh, with the tang of salt still sharp in its tendrils.

He drives to the sea each night, because the fever has caused his body to separate itself from his mind, as a defense mechanism perhaps. The result, however, is that his conception of the world he inhabits has veered so far away from the experience of his body in that world, that he has achieved a sort of ecstatic optimism, which is in no way grounded in what most of his colleagues insist on calling reality. He is buoyant with hope, on his drive to the sea.

And when he arrives, he strips off his sweat-soaked clothing and steps into the still-warm waters, thrilling to the brush and sway of the plants against his naked skin. Sometimes there is a moon above, and other times, all he sees are stars. Whatever the source of the light, he lays himself open to it, photosynthesizing as best as he is able at this late point in his life. The energy produced—frisson, spark, charge—is his alone, and he hoards it against the endless lassitude of coming days.

While the Paradise Hotel is in Manila, it is not in the Philippines. It has no address and it is quite difficult to find, except for the people who are already on their way there. Who have been invited. For them, it is impossible not to find the Paradise Hotel.

The men who stay at the Paradise Hotel, and they are always men, are like the ants in a field of long grass. They climb the blade nearest to them, look around, and realize that the blade they are climbing is not the blade they are meant to be on. And while the blades have not been artificially sharpened, they retain the ability to slice through skin all the way to the bone.

So the men in the Paradise Hotel must be careful. And careful they are. Because the men in the Paradise Hotel are not here to die. Not yet. They have not come this far—because some of them come from half the world away, just for this, for these moments of climbing, of surveying, of epiphany and despair—to lose their footing and bleed out here, on the multicolored carpet of an unnumbered room at the Paradise Hotel.

The Paradise Hotel employs a tattoo artist, although most of the men who come here do not get tattoos. Would not consider it. For the ones who do, however, consider it, there is quite a gauntlet to be run. The tattoo artist—he has long black hair and a wispy beard, dark eyes and a steady hand—says that he knows within five minutes of a client's appearance whether he will do the work.

Because the client must deserve the work just as the work must benefit the client. And for those worried about pain, about permanence, about regret, the tattoo artist sends them on their way. For there are other tattoo artists in the world who are all too happy to spill their ink on any paying customer. The tattoo artist at the Paradise Hotel will counsel restraint and forbearance, will advocate for hesitation and second thoughts. And then he will take the client by the hand and he will walk him to the door that leads out of the studio. It is not the same door that leads in. That was one of the conditions the tattoo artist placed upon the Paradise Hotel before he accepted the contract.

When the disappointed and confused client is shown the door by the tattoo artist, he re-enters the public spaces of the Paradise Hotel. There are many things to do here, but very few of the guests have any interest in doing them. Instead of visiting the gym or the indoor swimming pool or even the hair salon, the men who stay at the Paradise Hotel shuttle from room to room, discussing matters in low tones. Each of them has the undying belief that what they are doing at this very minute could affect the course of the world to come.

As do we all. Although not all of us stay at the Paradise Hotel, which exists only insofar as it is imagined by those of us not invited as guests. Just as our skin is marked only by the absence of tattoos from the tattoo artist who occupies the penthouse of the Paradise Hotel. Just as we are unmarked, so, too, we begin to exist in our imagining of the men who come and sometimes go, always disappointed with the lack of finality that they had imagined would be their portion of things in this world. Of course, none of us receive that, not even when we are worthy. If there is one thing we will always lack, it is a satisfactory ending.

—◇—

Contributors.

Leyna Krow *(Sinkhole)* is the author of the short story collection *I'm Fine, But You Appear to Be Sinking*. Her fiction has previously appeared in *Hayden's Ferry Review*, *Ninth Letter*, *South Dakota Review*, *Prairie Schooner*, *Santa Monica Review*, and other publications. She has an MFA from Eastern Washington University, and lives in Spokane, WA.

Sonya Chung *(Summer 1984)* is the author of the novels *Long for This World* and *The Loved Ones*, a staff writer for *The Millions*, and founding editor of *Bloom*. Sonya is a graduate of the MFA program in creative writing at the University of Washington and lived in Seattle for over seven years—during which time she came of age as a writer, reader, backpacker, snowboarder, gardener, and dog-mom. Sonya currently calls New York City home, while teaching fiction writing in upstate New York and working on her third novel, which takes place in the Pacific Northwest.

Born in Astoria, Oregon, **Eric Wagner** *(The Monolith)* holds a Ph.D. in biology from the University of Washington for his work on Magellanic penguins in Argentina. A regular contributor to *Orion* magazine and *High Country News*, his essays and journalism have also appeared in *Audubon*, *Smithsonian*, *Slate*, and *Cosmos*, among others. He currently lives in Seattle.

Michael Upchurch *(The Widower Muse)* grew up in England, the Netherlands and New Jersey, and has lived in Seattle since 1986. His novels include *Passive Intruder*, *The Flame Forest*, and *Air*, and his short stories have appeared in *Conjunctions*, *Glimmer Train*, and *The Seattle Review*, among others. He was a staff book critic for *The Seattle Times* for ten years (1998–2008) and has written extensively about books and the arts for other publications, including *The New York Times Book Review*, *Chicago Tribune*, *Washington Post* and *The American Scholar*. He is married to film critic John Hartl.

Anca Szilágyi *(Don't Worry)* is a Brooklynite living in Seattle. Her fiction and essays have appeared in *Electric Literature*, *Gastronomica*, *The Rumpus*, *Fairy Tale Review*, *Washington City Paper*, *Jewish in Seattle*, *Kirkus*, and elsewhere. Hailed by *The Stranger* as one of the "fresh new faces in Seattle fiction," she is the recipient of fellowships and awards from Made at Hugo House, Jack Straw Cultural Center, 4Culture, and Artist Trust.

Tiffany Midge *(The Jimmy Report)* has published fiction and nonfiction in *As/Us*, *Hinchas de Poesia*, *The Raven Chronicles*, *Yellow Medicine Review*, *Sovereign Bodies*, *Quarterly West*, and others. The 2012 recipient of the Kenyon Review Earthworks Prize for Indigenous Poetry and recipient of the Diane Decorah Memorial Poetry Award, she holds an MFA from the University of Idaho and currently serves as the Poet Laureate of Moscow, Idaho. Her poetry collection *Outlaws, Renegades and Saints: Diary of a Mixed-up Halfbreed* was published by Greenfield Review Press, and her poetry collection *The Woman Who Married a Bear* is forthcoming from the University of New Mexico Press. She is an enrolled member of the Standing Rock Sioux Tribe.

Kelly Froh *(Senior Time)* was born in Sheboygan, Wisconsin, and graduated from Emily Carr University of Art & Design with a BFA in Fine Arts. She's self-published numerous mini-comics and zines, including the all-comics magazine "The Weeknight Casserole Collection" and the Ignatz-nominated "Stew Brew" (in collaboration with her partner Max Clotfelter). Her comics have appeared in *Seattle Weekly*, *Poetry Northwest*, and *The Women's Review of Books*. Currently an art and creative writing teacher with Seniors Creating Art and WITS (Writers in the Schools), Kelly has performed at the Hugo House's acclaimed Literary Series, Gridlords, Lit Crawl, Pecha Kucha, On the Boards, APRIL, Spark Central, and at Bumbershoot. Kelly is also the co-founder and Executive Director of

Short Run Comix & Arts Festival, and in 2015 was nominated for a James W. Ray Venture Project Award.

Gina Williams *(Splitting the Sun)* is a Pacific Northwest native originally from Whidbey Island, Washington. Her writing and visual art have been featured by *Okey-Panky*, *Carve*, *The Boiler Journal*, *The Sun*, *Fugue*, and *tNY Press*, among others. Over the years, she has worked as a firefighter, reporter, housekeeper, caregiver, veterinarian's assistant, tree planter, gas station attendant, technical writer, cocktail waitress, and berry picker. She earned a Master's in Communications from the University of Oregon.

Kjerstin Johnson *(Alabama)* is a writer and editor living in Portland, Oregon. The former editor-in-chief of *Bitch* magazine, she has been published in *UTNE Reader* and *Bear Deluxe*, among others. She currently teaches at Portland State University.

Leah Sottile *(This is Meant to Hurt You)* is a writer and journalist. Her work has been featured by *The Washington Post*, *The Atlantic*, *Portland Monthly*, *Vice*, *Playboy*, *Broadly*, and *Al Jazeera America*, among others. She contributed a comic strip on First Amendment issues to the Comic Book Legal Defense Fund's *2013 Liberty Annual*, and her short fiction work has appeared in *Spokane Shorties*, *The Spokesman-Review*, and more. She lives in Portland, Oregon.

Monet Patrice Thomas *(A Multiplicity of Gray)* is a writer and poet who currently lives in Idaho. Her work has been published in *Hobart*, *Nailed*, *Knockout Poetry*, *Arcadia Magazine*, *Cobalt Review*, and *Word Riot*, among others. Born in Virginia and raised in North Carolina, she holds an MFA in Creative Writing from the Inland Northwest Center for Writers at Eastern Washington University in Spokane, Washington.

Chris McCann *(Unplace)* has been published in *SmokeLong Quarterly*, *Pedestal Magazine*, *Salt Hill Review*, and *Noctua Review*. He lives on Bainbridge Island.

Moss was founded by **Connor Guy**, an associate editor at a publishing house in New York City, and **Alex Davis-Lawrence**, a filmmaker and creative producer based in Los Angeles. Both were born and raised in Seattle.

—<o>—

Moss: Volume Two

Editors
Connor Guy
Alex Davis-Lawrence

Manager of Outreach
Amy Wilson

Contributing Editors
Sharma Shields
Michael Chin
M. Allen Cunningham
Elisabeth Sherman
Diana Xin

Photo Credits.

"A Residential Area of Portland," p. 46. 1973. Local identifier 412-DA-5625, Still Picture Records, Special Media Archives Services Division (NWCS-S), U.S. National Archives. Public domain.
Source: http://arcweb.archives.gov/arc/action/ExternalIdSearch?id=548112

"Old Houses, Portland, Oregon," p. 51. 1967. John Atherton. Available under a Creative Commons Attribution-ShareAlike 2.0 Generic license (CC BY-SA 2.0).
Source: https://www.flickr.com/photos/gbaku/763331239/

"State Police in N East Portland," p. 54. 1973. Local identifier 412-DA-12995, Still Picture Records, Special Media Archives Services Division (NWCS-S), U.S. National Archives. Public domain.
Source: http://arcweb.archives.gov/arc/action/ExternalIdSearch?id=555447

"Interior of Union Terminal, Portland," p. 61. 1974. Local identifier 412-DA-13679, Still Picture Records, Special Media Archives Services Division (NWCS-S), U.S. National Archives. Public domain.
Source: http://research.archives.gov/description/556131

"Portland, Oregon at night," p. 67. 1974. John Atherton. Available under a Creative Commons Attribution-ShareAlike 2.0 Generic license (CC BY-SA 2.0).
Source: https://www.flickr.com/photos/gbaku/2454141229/

"Amanita muscaria, two views of a mushroom, Hillsboro, Oregon," p. 112. 1910. Identifier CSB33099, The Field Museum Library. Public domain.
Source: https://www.flickr.com/photos/field_museum_library/4587524874/

"Storm clouds over James Island, La Push," p.117. 1963. Identifier LIN0394, Lawrence D. Lindsley Photographs, University of Washington Libraries. Available under a Creative Commons Attribution 2.0 Generic license (CC BY 2.0).
Source: http://content.lib.washington.edu/u?/ll,1321

"Comb Tooth mushroom plant specimens growing on tree bark, displayed on a table, Hillsboro, Oregon," p. 121. 1910. Identifier CSB33065, The Field Museum Library. Public domain.
Source: https://www.flickr.com/photos/field_museum_library/4586899557/

"Orchard District, Wenatchee River, near Cashmere, Washington," p. 144. 1920. Identifier 299173, Records of the Forest Service, U.S. National Archives. Public domain.
Source: https://catalog.archives.gov/id/299173

"Farm buildings and orchards at Eckert's ranch, Washington," p.148. 1904. Identifier BAR189, Albert Henry Barnes Photographs, University of Washington Libraries. Public domain.
Source: http://content.lib.washington.edu/u?/barnes,206

"Fishermen horse seining for salmon on the Columbia River," p.153. Date unknown. Identifier COB113, John N. Cobb Photographs, University of Washington Libraries. Public domain.
Source: http://content.lib.washington.edu/u?/cobb,99

"Irrigating a 5-year-old winesap orchard near North Yakima," p. 157. 1918. Internet Archive Book Images, U.S. Department of Agriculture, National Agricultural Library. Public domain.
Source: https://www.flickr.com/photos/internetarchivebookimages/14577513050/

"Columbia River, Washington," p.184. 1913. Identifier BAR022, Albert Henry Barnes Photographs, University of Washington Libraries. Public domain.
Source: http://content.lib.washington.edu/u?/barnes,155

"Bluffs along Columbia River," p. 189. Date unknown. Item Number P217:set 025 008, Oregon State University Special Collections. Public domain.
Source: https://www.flickr.com/photos/osucommons/3679661394/

"The Glaciers of Mount Tacoma," p. 193. 1883. Internet Archive Book Images, Harold B. Lee Library, Brigham Young University. Public domain.
Source: https://www.flickr.com/photos/internetarchivebookimages/14758574742/

—◦—

Acknowledgments.

There are many, many generous and passionate people to thank for the continued success of *Moss*. To our readers and subscribers, our staff and writers, our friends and family—thank you for helping us get through another year, and for making this Volume even more exciting than the last. Your consistent support fuels everything that we do, and is emblematic of the vitality and sense of community that keeps the Northwest writing scene innovative and important. We're especially grateful to our Patrons, whose exceptional support made this anthology possible:

Max Boyd
Alba Conte
Diane Davis
Ronnie-Gail Emden
Joan Flores
Naomi Gibbs
Paul Lawrence and Cynthia Jones
Tod Marshall
Chris McCann
Colleen McMonagle and Anthony Peters
Ilana Woods

—◦—

Interested in subscribing?
Visit mosslit.com to support Northwest writing and
get the annual print edition delivered to your door.